OVERHEARD

AND QUOTED

"Out Of Context"

Collected by SJ Hills

From jazz bars to seedy clubs

From coffee shops to clip joints

From bars to bistros

Overheard in old Soho

This Work First Published In 2009
by Century17 Publishing, London.
www.century-17.com

This paperback edition first published in 2009

Typeset by Century17 Publishing.

All rights reserved.
© Copyright, S J Hills, 2009

This book is sold subject to the condition that it shall not, by way of trade or otherwise, be lent, resold, hired out or otherwise circulated without the publisher's prior consent in any form of binding or cover other than that in which it is published, and without a subsequent condition including this condition being imposed on the subsequent purchaser.

First Edition. Revision I-VIII
ISBN 978-0-9559921-4-8

Cover artwork by the author. © Copyright 2009

Century17 Publishing
Restoring classics from the past
Rewriting classics for the future

Other Titles by S J Hills.

Scarborough Fair.
(Restoration Comedy style drama based on *The Relapse* by Vanbrugh – considered too risqué to be performed for over 200 years)

To Take A Wife.
(Restoration Comedy style drama based on *The Country Wife* by Wycherley – famously banned from print for almost 200 years and considered too outrageous to be performed at all)

Wishing Well.
(Restoration Comedy style drama based on *Epsom Wells* by the Poet Laureate, *Shadwell*. Long forgotten and out of print due to lewdness, this wonderful play had a fine balance of bawdiness with delicious satire and biting wit)

Love In A Nunnery.
(Restoration Comedy style drama based on *The Assignation* by *Dryden*. Humour, bawdiness, scheming, cunning and wit, with a serious underlying theme still just as relevant today. Can the power of love overcome all obstacles?)

Great Fairy Tales of the World. Vol. 1
Dramatised in English for Encyclopaedia Britannica Japan.

Great Fairy Tales of the World. Vol. 2
Dramatised in English for Encyclopaedia Britannica Japan.

The Star Crossed Lovers.
(*Romeo and Juliet* faithfully translated line-by-line for modern audiences and education)

She Who Would Be King.
(*Macbeth* faithfully translated line-by-line for modern audiences and education)

For further titles and information visit www.century-17.com

I was quoted "Out Of Context"

In the bars, coffee houses, clubs, stores, galleries, and streets of Old Soho

That one casual line caught out of time and place from the rest of the conversation, leaving the line to take on a whole new depth, meaning, and sometimes mystery of its own in an often humourous or disturbing way.

Poignant, enigmatic, often informative, always random.

The person rushing past in the street on their phone, that moment of unexpected silence in a crowded place when a single voice rings out before being lost again to the background chatter.

The time of night when the drink has flowed freely and the tongue has loosened, or the heartfelt frustrations of the day being vented in a vain attempt to be rid of them.

A pearl of wisdom let loose into the ether to be lost forever. Until now that is. no attempt has been made to make them understandable, let them stand alone on their own merit. They come when you least expect them, just as in life.

Maybe one of them was yours.

Every book needs a gripping opening paragraph to draw the reader in.
This has it all: naked, prostrate, braying, massage, millionairess...

I do have a penis,
It's just attached to someone else's body.

He made the ultimate sacrifice one man can make for another
He ran off with my wife. One day I must thank him.

At my mum's house, we were asked by a pop-up
"How many cocks can one bitch handle?"

Are vegans allowed to swallow?

Mindful of my five portions of fruit and veg a day
I put an extra slice of lemon in my vodka

I went to a wife swapping party once
And I wasn't even married!

It's one of the great philosophical questions of our age
On a par with David's: "Should gays be allowed in male changing rooms?"

The best part of being dumped is you are now available to 50% of the world's population.
That's rather a lot of people. One of them has got to want to have kinky sex with you.

I have had depression
It's almost the same as being sober.

Next time I say hello I will stare at your cleavage
like all the others do

She's easy on the eye, and not too taxing on the brain

I had my biggest one ever on the top deck of a London bus.

I put off and put off getting married.
Then one day I got pissed and said yes. Only it wasn't to my girlfriend.

It doesn't matter how beautiful or sexy she looks
Some mug somewhere is fed up taking her shit

Tell the truth to yourself, then will you know the true you.
But don't tell it to anyone else, they won't want to know you.

Nothing gets people more animated than an Apple product.
It's like Marmite. Those that love it, love it, those that hate it spit fire
and fury at what is in essence an inanimate object.
I quite like Marmite.

Having friends is an old fashioned concept from the 20th
century
I am lucky that I was born early enough to experience the fad, prior to
the conception of the virtual world.

I have never borrowed money,
Except for once when I borrowed a fiver off a mate, so I guess I have,
but I paid it back, so my credit rating shouldn't be affected.

You try so hard to be interesting
and fail so convincingly every time

I KNOW IT SAYS 'LOVE THY NEIGHBOUR' IN THE BIBLE
BUT YOU'VE TAKEN IT A BIT TOO LITERALLY

HE STOOD THERE NAKED AND ASKED IF I WANTED SAUSAGES
ALL I KEPT THINKING WAS: "PRICK WITH A FORK"

HE CAN'T BE GAY,
THERE'S NO CLOSET, BIG ENOUGH FOR HIM TO BE IN.

HE JUST PHONED, HE'S WASTED.
HE'S IN A CAB AND HE CAN'T REMEMBER WHERE HE LIVES.

MUM, WHAT DOES 'BLOODY WANKER' MEAN?

SHE WAS A BELLY DANCER AND COULD MOVE IN WAYS
THAT WERE BOTH UNEXPECTED AND WELCOME ALL AT THE SAME TIME.

I'VE GOT A DELIVERY, DO YOU HAVE A BACK ENTRANCE?

IT WAS YOUR ARSE THAT WAS PHOTOCOPIED WASN'T IT?
I RECOGNISED THE SPOTS.

I ONCE ASKED A GIRL OUT BECAUSE SHE WAS A DEPECHE MODE FAN.

MY HISTORY PROFESSOR WAS OLD AND UGLY
I'M STILL NOT SURE WHY I FANCIED HIM. I'D PROBABLY STILL THROW IT TO HIM.

ORAL SKILLS ARE ALWAYS A GOOD THING TO TEACH YOUNG LADIES

YOU COME WITH WHO YOU WANT TO LEAVE WITH
BUT LEAVE WITH WHO YOU WANT TO COME WITH.

I HAVE LOTS OF THINGS TO DO.
I JUST CAN'T DECIDE WHICH ONE FIRST, THEN I THINK I CAN START ANYTIME BECAUSE I DO NOT HAVE TO END ANYTIME, THEN I THINK A CUP OF COFFEE WOULD BE NICE, AFTER THAT IT ALL FALLS INTO A STEADY DECLINE OF PROCRASTINATION.

I RECOMMEND THE SANDWICH PLACE BY THE POND.
THEY ARE NICE AND THEY INVITE YOU TO SIT BY THE POND AND THE GEESE STEAL YOUR FOOD.

A MEATBALL SANDWICH DOES SOUND WROUGHT WITH PROBLEMS.

GINGER HAIR IS NOT A DISABILITY YOU CRUEL BASTARD.

YOU SHOULD STICK A BULB OF MERCURY ON THE END
THEN YOU'D HAVE AN EXCUSE FOR STICKING IT IN EVERYONE'S MOUTHS AND BOTTOMS.

SHORT SPEECHES ALWAYS GO DOWN WELL
NO MATTER WHAT IS SAID

A HICCUP, A BELCH, A STUPID GRIN AND SLIDING UNDER THE TABLE
IT DOES HAVE SOMETHING GOING FOR IT

I THINK I WILL START MY BEST MAN'S SPEECH WITH;
 "YOU'RE PROBABLY WONDERING WHY I'VE GATHERED YOU ALL HERE TODAY..."
THEN GO ROUND THE ROOM IN A POIROT STYLE, POINTING OUT ALL THOSE WHO HAVE HAD 'PREVIOUS EXPERIENCE' OF THE BRIDE, THEN ALL THOSE ABOUT TO HAVE 'SUBSEQUENT EXPERIENCE', WHILE HANDING OUT A PRICE LIST FOR HER SERVICES.

WHATEVER HAPPENED TO THE GOOD OLD DAYS OF ROMANCE, EH?
CLUBBING THEM OVER THE BACK OF THE HEAD AND DRAGGING THEM BACK TO THE CAVE TO DEBAUCH THEM.
AND IF YOU GOT A DODGY ONE YOU COULD ALWAYS THROW IT BACK.

THIS IS WHAT KARAOKE WAS MADE FOR
UNINTENTIONAL HUMOUR AND HUMILITY.

LUNCH FOR HER IS A COW SANDWICHED BETWEEN TWO BREAD VANS.

I WOULD LIKE TO MAKE WILD PASSIONATE LOVE
IT'S LIKE RAPE, BUT WITH MORE FILLING AND LESS STRUGGLING

I'LL RAM THAT ICE CREAM VAN UP YOUR ARSE

FROM NOW ON I'M ONLY GOING TO HAVE SEX WITH MY BOYFRIEND.

I USED TO GO OUT WITH A GIRL WITH EPILEPSY
I ASKED HER WHAT I WOULD DO IF SHE HAD ONE ON THE JOB, AS THAT'S QUITE
COMMON. SHE SAID "TRY AND HOLD ON, AND GOOD LUCK"

THERE IS AN EX BRITISH CHAMPION BOXER WHO DRINKS IN MY LOCAL.
HE IS A LOVELY CHAP AND A REAL GENTLEMAN, BUT THIS IS ALSO THE MAN WHO GOT
HIS HEAD STUCK IN HIS BICYCLE NOT VERY LONG AGO.

DARTS IS THE ONLY SPORT I HAVE THE FIGURE FOR.

HAPPY SACKS SEEKS FUN BAGS FOR NIGHT OF JOY

CUT A COCK SHAPE OUT OF PAPER
AND REST IT ON A SUNBATHING PERSON.

A GREY STREAK IN THE PUBES ALWAYS REMINDS ME OF A BADGER

DUNNO WHY I WORK,
MY ONLY AMBITION IN LIFE IS TO BE A CHAMPAGNE GUZZLING TROPHY WIFE

I THOUGHT YOU WERE IN THE UNMARRIED STAGES OF BEING MARRIED

YOU HAVE REACHED THE BOTTOMLESS DEPTHS OF THE PIT OF DESPAIR.

I THINK I'LL GET MINE OUT.

I WAS WEARING A LITTLE BLACK DRESS
WHICH HE KNEW CONCEALED A FANTASTIC PAIR OF TITS

IT IS NEVER APPROPRIATE NOT TO USE LUBE

YOU'RE NOT SUCKING ME INTO TELLING MY DIRTY SECRETS.
NOT WITH HALF A PINT OF CIDER. OH NO, IT'LL TAKE A LOT MORE THAN THAT.

THEY ARE NOT HER LEGS

CAN YOUR GIRLFRIEND DO THIS?

IF ONLY HE WAS MAN ENOUGH TO HAVE PUSHED HIM

BLOW-UP SHEEP WITH 'REAR ENTRY ORIFICE'?
AM I THE ONLY ONE THAT FINDS THIS DIFFICULT TO UNDERSTAND?

COWBOYS AREN'T FARMERS

IS IT YOU DOING THAT?
PUT YOUR HANDS WHERE WE CAN SEE THEM.

I AM LISTENING INTENTLY TO MY WIFE TELLING ME HOW LATE IT IS.
I AM WELL PRACTICED IN THE ART OF IGNORING.

I DIDN'T COME SO IT'S NOT CHEATING.

JUST READING THAT MADE ME CROSS MY LEGS

I'VE HEARD OF PEOPLE LOOKING LIKE THEIR DOGS.
THIS IS EVEN WORSE.

MY TOASTER IS DOING STRANGE THINGS WITH BREAD
THAT MY SMOKE ALARM DISAGREES WITH.

IT WAS A STOLEN POLICE CAR
I DON'T KNOW THE MAKE OF THE CAR THOUGH.

YOURS IS MUCH MORE MINIMALIST THAN MINE

MY APOLOGIES FOR BEING THE MILLIONTH PERSON
TO THINK I WAS BEING FUNNY AND ORIGINAL.

I WANT A CAR WITH BALLS
WITH THE KIND OF ENGINE A GIRL WANTS TO TAKE HOME AND STRADDLE.

ARE YOU WELSH?
YOU SHOULD BE

WITH ALL THE PILLS YOU POP
DO YOUR PANTS RATTLE LIKE A BAG OF SKITTLES WHEN YOU WALK?

I WAS INTO THE SAME WOMAN AS ANOTHER MAN ONCE

I DON'T UNDERSTAND
WHY ALL PEOPLE NOT OF CAUCASIAN DESCENT HAVE BLACK HAIR.

HE'S LIKE ALL THE THINGS I HATE MOST
ALL ROLLED INTO ONE.

WE MUST ALL BE VERY QUIET
AND NOT LET ANYBODY SEE US

YOU MEAN GULLIBLE'S NOT IN THE DICTIONARY?

THE PACKAGING ON THIS ONE SAYS ALASKA
SO I GUESS IT'S COVERED IN PETROL OR SOMETHING

I JUST COVERED MY MOUTH AND GASPED IN HORROR.
AND SAID "FUCKING HELL" A LOT.

I THINK SHE'S ONE OF THE MOST BEAUTIFUL PEOPLE EVER.
I FANCY HER MORE THAN MOST MEN. AND I'M A GIRL WHO REALLY LIKES COCK.

FUCK-ME EYES
THAT'S WHAT SHE HAS.

SACKED AFTER 20 MINUTES?
WHAT DID YOU DO? TURN UP FOR A PLASTERER'S ASSISTANT JOB WEARING A SUIT?

APPARENTLY SHE'S SOMEONE ELSE AS WELL NOW

NO! IT HURT TOO MUCH LAST TIME

TAKE ONE SOCK OFF A DRUNK SLEEPER
AND PUT IT OVER THE TOP OF THEIR OTHER SOCK. THEY'LL LOOK FOR THE MISSING SOCK FOR HOURS

MINE ARE TOO SMALL
AND MY VAGINA IS NOT MADE OF PLASTIC.

I STILL LIKE KISSING.
COCK STUFF IS FUN, BUT KISSING IS JUST AS GOOD.

YOU LOOK LIKE SOMEONE SURPRISED YOU FROM BEHIND

ALL OF US PUT TOGETHER
WOULD HAVE NO CHANCE AGAINST YOU

THE E, S, AND X KEYS ARE WEARING OUT ON MY LAPTOP.
WHY THOSE THREE?
OH. YOU KNOW WHAT, THAT WASN'T ACTUALLY WHY.

THAT'S HOW I WALK EVERYWHERE.
WITH A SWOOSH AND A GALLOP!

NO AMOUNT OF TITTAGE
WOULD MAKE ANYONE NAMED "VELMA" ATTRACTIVE.

DOES IT COUNT AS POO-ING OUTDOORS
IF YOU HAD A HOUSE WITH AN OUTSIDE TOILET?

MY DAD DOES THAT
I WISH HE WOULDN'T

YOU NEED CHEMICAL HELP, MY FRIEND

I PUT THEM UP MY BOTTOM

I'VE GOT A HOT CROSS BUN THAT I WARMED UP ON THE RADIATOR.

JUST TO CLEAR THE AIR OF ALL THE HATRED HERE,
I'M GOING TO TALK ABOUT FOOTBALL.

I'M NOT GINGER, I'M BLACK-HAIRED.

WHY DOES SNOT TURN YELLOW-GREEN WHEN YOU'RE ILL?

I HATE OLDER MEN KEEP TRYING IT ON WITH ME,
EVEN AFTER I SAY "LOOK, I HAVE A BOYFRIEND AND YOU ARE THIRTEEN YEARS OLDER THAN ME AND I SUPPORT LIVERPOOL".

I LOVE THE IRONY.
EVEN IF IT'S NOT ACTUAL IRONY.

I GAVE HIM MY MATE'S ADDRESS AS MY POST KEEPS GETTING STOLEN.
HE WENT TO HER HOUSE TO PICK ME UP AND NOW THEY'RE GETTING MARRIED.

I WENT TO UNI IN THE USA
MY FIRST DAY I ASKED TO BORROW A RUBBER. NOT EVEN AS A JOKE. NOT A GREAT START.

MY BOYFRIEND DOESN'T DO EITHER OF THOSE
HENCE I'M WAITING FOR THE APPROPRIATE MOMENT TO CHUCK HIM.

BUT VIBRATORS DON'T TALK TO YOU, OR BUY YOU FOOD, OR PRESENTS.

I HAVE HAD GOATS
ONE CHOKED ON A DOUGHNUT AND DIED AND ANOTHER GOT RUN OVER BY A TRAIN.
I WENT OFF THEM AFTER THAT.

IS THERE A POLITE WAY TO ASK SOMEONE TO GET TESTED
FOR SEXUALLY TRANSMITTED DISEASES BEFORE THEY SLEEP WITH YOU?

SHE STRUTS SEXILY
BUT SHE HAS ARMS LIKE A MAN AND GUZZLES LAGER

MORNING WOOD?
IN THE EVENING?

BIROS SEEM TO DISAPPEAR
AND AN EQUAL NUMBER OF EXTRA METAL COAT HANGERS APPEAR IN THEIR PLACE.

MY LOCAL LAUNDERETTE IS SHIT.
TOOK OVER AN HOUR FOR THE MACHINE TO NOT DRY MY LAUNDRY.

YOU'VE SEEN ONE NAKED LADY, YOU'VE SEEN THEM ALL.
I MEAN, IT'S NOT LIKE ARSES LOOK ALL THAT DIFFERENT.

IN HER TRACKSUIT DANCING ROUND HER FAKE HANDBAG
WITH A BOTTLE OF ALCOPOPS SHOWING OFF HER WOBBLY MIDRIFF, FAT THIGHS,
CAMEL TOE AND PIERCINGS WHILE CHEWING GUM.

IMAGINE BEING STOPPED IN THE STREET
AND ASKED IF YOU'RE HIM OUT OF STATUS QUO. THE HORROR.

SCOTLAND... ISN'T THAT IN ENGLAND?

THANK YOU FOR TELLING US THIS
YOU MAY NOW CRAWL BACK TO WHEREVER YOU CAME FROM.

EMOTIONAL BAGGAGE IS A BASTARD TO CARRY AROUND
BUT I MANAGE

I HAD SOME NONCY ORGANIC FRUITY PORRIDGE THING
THAT I BOUGHT IN A MOMENT OF 'OOO! PRETTY PACKAGING' MADNESS.

IT'S AS IF MILLIONS OF SPERM
SUDDENLY CRIED OUT IN TERROR AND WERE THEN JUST AS SUDDENLY SILENCED.

I OFTEN MISJUDGE HOW MUCH
I SHOULD INFORM THE BOYFRIEND ABOUT WHAT I AM THINKING.

BECAUSE I WON'T SWALLOW?

I TEND TO UNDERESTIMATE THE QUANTITY OF RICE NEEDED TO COOK
AND OVERESTIMATE THE AMOUNT OF CHILLI TO GO WITH IT

DID YOU KNOCK UP THREE OF THE SECRETARIES
BY THE CARELESS SPRAYING ABOUT OF YOUR GENETIC MATERIAL?

SHE HAS A FANNY LIKE A RIPPED OUT FIREPLACE

I REWOUND THE TAPE AND PRESSED PLAY,
EXPECTING TO HEAR THAT WONDERFUL OPENING MUSIC. ALL I GOT WAS DIRTY, DIRTY PORN.

WHERE WOULD WE BE
IF EVERYONE GAVE UP ON THINGS JUST BECAUSE THEY ARE UNPLEASANT AND SHIT?

HOW DARE YOU SPEND MY TAXES ON YOUR DEBAUCHED SOCIAL LIFE

SERVES YOU RIGHT FOR SUNBATHING IN DECEMBER

I TIED A PLANK TO MY ARSE

WHAT KIND OF FOOL ARE YOU?
TRYING TO UNDERSTAND A WOMAN'S THOUGHT PATTERNS.

I THOUGHT THAT WAS UNIVERSALLY CALLED A 'TITFUCK'

BLOODY HELL!
THEY'RE SHAGGING AND EVERYTHING!

I'M READING HIS STORIES ABOUT HIS SEX LIFE
THEY REALLY ARE VERY FUNNY. ALTHOUGH I AM SURE HE NEVER INTENDED THEM AS HUMOUR WHEN HE WROTE THEM.

I'VE SEEN THE 'BOING' ACTION

THE THRILL OF FINDING OUT WHAT HAPPENS
WHEN YOU SIT DOWN ON A COKE BOTTLE.

YOU CAN, JUST NOT WITH MASSIVE ACCURACY,
BUT THEN AGAIN NOR CAN MOST MEN

THREADING YOUR FINGERS THROUGH THEIR HAIR
AND JUST AS THEY PULL AWAY, PULL THEM IN AGAIN FOR ANOTHER DEEP KISS.
IT'S THE POWER THING, LIKE SAYING WE'RE NOT STOPPING TILL I SAY SO.

I'VE NO REASON NOT TO BELIEVE HIM.
IT'S A LOT MORE ENTERTAINING THAN SOMEONE NOT PISSING ON THE BLARNEY STONE.

I GENTLY SUCK THE BOTTOM LIP OUT AS I PULL AWAY.
DRIVES MY NAN WILD.

I LOVE A GOOD SNOG,
IT'S SOMETHING I ALWAYS ASSOCIATE WITH FANTASTIC SEX.

THE ONLY WOMEN I'VE KISSED THIS YEAR
ARE ME MUM AND ME GRAN

HE COULD PUT A SMILE ON THE MOTHER OF THE BRIDE'S LIPS

I NOW REMEMBER
WHY I FELT USED THE LAST TIME I GAVE HER ANOTHER CHANCE

I BET HE'S BEEN PRACTICING THAT ONE IN THE MIRROR

I'VE NEVER HAD AN STD
AND I'VE NOT ALWAYS BEEN A GOOD GIRL EITHER

FLOWERS ARE TOKENS FOR THE COCK WASH

MY BOYFRIEND CAN'T WORK OUT WHY THE TV REMOTE
NEEDS NEW BATTERIES SO OFTEN.

I BET HE TASTES LIKE HADDOCK CORNETTOS

I THINK SHE'S JUST LED A SHELTERED LIFE

THIS VIOLATES THE INJUNCTION YOU KNOW

WHAT HAS COCAINE GOT TO DO WITH HURRYING UP?

IF EVERYBODY HAD THAT MANY FIRST NAMES
THERE WOULDN'T BE ENOUGH TO GO ROUND

MAKE HER EAT IT ON HER CORNFLAKES

MY WIFE PUT THE WHOLE CORNET IN HER MOUTH IN ONE GO.
THAT'S WHEN I KNEW I HAD TO MARRY HER.

THERE ARE SOME THINGS I JUST DON'T NEED TO KNOW

RED HAIR THAT IS - MY EYES ARE GREENISH

ONE BEAUTIFUL SUNDAY MORNING CHURCHGOERS WERE TREATED TO
THE SIGHT OF ME TAKING THE RUBBISH OUT WITH MY FLIES OPEN. THEN MY WIFE
POINTED OUT I HAD NO UNDERPANTS ON.

THAT IS EERILY SIMILAR TO WHAT MY HUSBAND SAYS
WHEN I WON'T PUT OUT

I ONCE PHONED THE LOCAL JEHOVAH'S AND LEFT A MESSAGE
SAYING THAT I HAD LAPSED AND LEFT MY EX'S NAME AND TELEPHONE NUMBER.

MAYBE SOME BUTTER FOR LUBRICATION

A LOT OF THE '70S WAS IN BLACK AND WHITE
THE '60S WAS IN COLOUR, BUT IN STRANGE HUES OF PYSCHODELIA
THE '50S WAS DARK.

CUT A 12 YEAR OLD'S FACE OFF
AND STITCH IT TO YOUR OWN. YOU ARE BEYOND WRINKLE CREAM

I LOVE A GOOD EXPERIMENT

NEVER TRUST A WOMAN WHOSE THIGHS HAVE NEVER MET.

PERFORATED YOUR OWN LUNG DURING AUTOFELLATIO?
AS CILLA WOULD SAY, THAT'S A LORRA, LORRA COCK.

I'VE HEARD YOU'RE A BIT DIRTY,
GO AND GET TESTED AND I MIGHT GIVE YOU A GO ON THESE

IT TASTES LIKE NAIL VARNISH REMOVER AND FIZZY SUGAR

I TOLD YOU BEFORE
NO, I WON'T SLEEP WITH YOU — OR STAY AWAKE!

I FEEL SORRY FOR HER HUSBAND
WE HANDCUFFED HIM NAKED TO THE BED AND THEN FUCKED OFF TO THE BEDROOM NEXT DOOR.

CAN SHE REMEMBER THE DAYS
WHEN SHE WASN'T STUCK IN THE LOO WITH HER HEAD DOWN THE BOWL?

LET'S GET SOME MORAL OUTRAGE OVER HERE!

I'M HAVING LUNCH WITH EMMA,
IT'S CALLED BECKS.

THE HOME OFFICE ARE PAYING ME TO GO OUT DRINKING
I'M HARDLY GOING TO REFUSE!

HAVE YOU LOOKED DOWN THE BACK OF THE SOFA?
I AM ALWAYS FINDING THINGS I'VE LOST DOWN THERE – NOT GIRLFRIENDS I ADMIT.

WE'VE ALL DONE THINGS WE REGRET
BUT I THINK YOURS MAY BE ON THE INTERNET.

I HOPE YOU STOOD ON THE PUPPY'S EARS –
SO IT COULDN'T GET ITS HEAD OFF THE GROUND

I'VE PERFECTED RIDING THE BENDY ONES

LAST NIGHT I WENT TO THE PUB
WHICH IS MUCH THE SAME AS I DID YESTERDAY AFTERNOON, EXCEPT IT WASN'T DARK.

YOU MAKE ME ALL MOIST WHEN YOU GET ALL SHOUTY

I KNOW THAT I DRANK WINE AND HAD A HAIR CUT.
THE REST IS A BLANK.

BEEN WITH THEM MAN AND BOY
AND NEVER ONCE HAD TO TOAST THE SOLES OF THE FEET OF ANY OF THE STAFF.

I SEE THAT WOMAN'S WEEKLY NEVER BRANCHED OUT
INTO MONTHLY PUBLICATIONS.

ALL THOSE STORIES YOU READ IN BOOKS BY CATHOLICS ARE RUBBISH
THERE WAS NOTHING SEXUALLY REPRESSED ABOUT THE BARMAID IN THE HOTEL I WAS IN.

THEY SPEND ALL THEIR MONIES
ON CIGARETTES, ALCOHOL, PET FOOD AND TRACKSUITS.

ALL I HEARD WAS
"BLAH BLAH BLAH, I'M AN ARROGANT CUNT"

I KNOW IT SOUNDS ABSURD
BUT I CUT MY NOSE WHILE SHAVING. DON'T ASK!

I THINK WE SHOULD EAT MORE HORSES

THEY ONLY LIVE THERE TO BE NEAR THE SAILORS
SO THEY CAN GET THEIR YARDARM OF SAILOR LENGTH EVERY FRIDAY DOWN THE DOCKS

When it started getting bigger I panicked.
I was thinking, whoah! Where is this thing going to stop!

Strictly speaking, HE wrestled me.
Actually ... 'strictly' speaking, he got me in a bear-hug, made some manly grunts, and then fell on his arse

I hate the smell of cold greasy chicken on my fingers

I called the Missus, "peanut"
Quick as a flash, she responded "but you're the one with the salty aftertaste." The humour exacerbated because we were sitting at her parent's dinner table at the time

Bantams give an egg so small
All you need do is whisper something filthy at it and it's cooked enough to dip your soldiers in

Go out into the back garden and dig up a plant and some turf put it in his lap and scream "now look what you've done!"
Then as he wakes up and opens his eyes, go upstairs to bed. He will be hours trying to figure out what he has done..

I won't play if you call me a slut

I'll be too drunk to go anywhere by five pm

All you'll succeed in doing
is putting me in a bad mood for the rest of the day

TOILET ATTENDANTS CAN KISS MY ARSE IF THEY WANT MONEY

WHERE IS THE FUCKING IDIOT ANYWAY?
WE'VE A ROASTING TO DO

IS THAT MARK ON YOUR FOREHEAD FROM THE HEADBOARD?

QUICK -- LET'S MAKE LOVE, BEFORE YOU DIE

IT TOOK SEVEN SHOWERS TO FEEL CLEAN AGAIN

I'VE GOT A CERTIFICATE TO PROVE IT!

HE'S REMARRYING MY MUM,
YOU'D THINK HE WOULD HAVE LEARNT HIS LESSON.

IT'S A BIT BIG
I PREFER A SNUGGER FIT

WHEN HE'S ASLEEP I LIE THERE WISHING HE'D STOP BREATHING,
NOT BECAUSE HE SNORES. I JUST HATE HIM.

DID YOU DO THE DIRTY?

I HAD TO TELL MY WIFE SHE WASN'T GOING TO BE MY WIFE ANYMORE

GET IT DOWN AS QUICK AS YOU CAN
DON'T SUCK ON IT FOR AGES

We already know men won't go to the doctor
In case he sticks things up their arse

Have you got an opening for a new husband then?

Life is never quiet and boring,
It has ways of kicking you in the teeth to make you appreciate being alive.

Apparently I've been middle aged for six years
Perhaps I should grow up

I remember when she was thin
And did the southern news with the baldy bloke

They eat away at your stomach you know

I know exactly what is called for,
A slinky low backed number with too much cleavage

You need the bad to appreciate the good.

It was fun, I'd go back there
I'm not sure my liver and brain would survive a second pass though

I never know whether to ask for a safe word
On a first date or not. I don't want to scare them off.

He is such a mummy's boy.
I make him cut and file my toenails

I'VE JUST DISCOVERED
I HAVE A FAKE BOYFRIEND

I BOUGHT SOME CHINESE WINGS
CHINESE CHICKENS MUST LOOK DIFFERENT TO ENGLISH ONES, THEY SURE TASTE DIFFERENT.

THE WORST NIGHT OUT IS
WAKING UP TO FIND SKID MARKS ON YOUR Y-FRONTS - ON THE OUTSIDE!

PLUNGE THEM IN HOT THEN COLD WATER REPEATEDLY
OR YOU COULD OF COURSE ALWAYS WEAR A CONDOM.

IF IT TURNS OUT YOU ARE
I'M NEVER SPEAKING TO YOU AGAIN

AND SOMEONE JUST HAD TO STEP IN IT

HE'S SUCH A HORNY BUGGER.
HE CAN'T KEEP HIS TONGUE TO HIMSELF.

FAB
THAT MAKES ME THIRTEEN AGAIN

DON'T COME THAT WITH ME
YOU HELD HER DOWN

YOU CAN
IF YOU SQUEEZE TIGHT ENOUGH

ITS GOT AN UNUSUAL TEXTURE
AND A SLIGHTLY NUTTY TASTE

I'D RATHER HAVE ANAL THAN WATCH CRICKET ANY DAY.

ONLY WHEN THE MOON IS FULL AND THE BLUE BULLS ARE RUNNING
IS IT BULLS OR BALLS?

ONE LIKES SHEEP
AND THE OTHER LIKES STRANGE MEN IN TOILETS

THE CONCEPT OF MARY BEING A HERMAPHRODITE
AND FERTILISING HERSELF IS MORE LIKELY THAN THE EXISTENCE OF A SUPREME BEING

I DON'T HAVE ONE
AND I WENT TO HIGH SCHOOL

DYSENTERY
NOW THAT'S A MAN'S CHOICE OF DEATH

ONE HAND ON THE ARSE
NO SQUEEZING.

I'VE GOT A THERMAL VEST ON TODAY
MY TORSO IS TOASTY

IT WILL MATTER.
IF YOU'RE NOT BENDY

I hate 'auto complete' sentencing on phones.
Especially when I accidentally send a message to the taxi company telling them I love them from the drunk train.

On the drunk train home it's not just kissing that goes on.
It's either bloody smelly burgers or badly wrapped kebabs.

No more embarrassment with odour or ballooning

One day I'll make you a champagne lush.
Then you'll know

Its more purist watching it fucked -
and more fun, if you can concentrate on it for long enough

You've got the lady horn more than usual today

I don't know what you're doing, but it feels nice

When my mum retires from being on the game
you can have a go.

I really get on well with women, they seem attracted to me
until it gets to the sleeping with me part.

I have woken up on trains
in parts of the country I didn't know existed.

I regularly get a taxi home for fifty quid
rather than wait for the 5 quid train. But I'm rich and usually drunk

I MAY AS WELL DIE NOW
THINGS COULDN'T GET ANY BETTER THAN RIGHT NOW

I'LL HAVE YOU SCREAMING SO LOUD
THE NEIGHBOURS WILL BE CALLING THE POLICE.

HE WON'T BE COMING, HE'S HAVING DAY SURGERY ON HIS 'ROIDS

THE PEOPLE THAT GET ON BUSES
ARE ENOUGH TO PUT YOU OFF EVER GETTING ON ONE.

I'VE BEEN A VERY NAUGHTY GIRL
I'LL BE WAITING IN MY ROOM FOR A GOOD SPANKING.

IF I FUCKED UP, PEOPLE MIGHT DIE

MY MUM IS A VIRGIN,
SHE SAYS BOTH ME AND MY BROTHER WERE IMMACULATELY 'CONCEALED'

IMMACULATE DECEPTION

YOU ARE MALE
THE WORLD IS YOUR TOILET

I TOLD HIM TO MAKE HIS GOAL A NEW CAR FOR MY 30TH BIRTHDAY,
HE MADE HIS GOAL THE NEW CZECH TEMP. BECAUSE SHE WAS HAPPY WITH SHOES.

IT'S A FAIR WATERFALL IN MY PANTS AFTER SEEING THAT

Mini skirts, 'tramp stamps' and sperm stained thighs.
A lovely place on a Saturday night

I asked the taxi driver if it ever stopped raining
He told me he had no idea as he had only lived here 15 years

I'm really not as much of a scrubber as this makes me sound.

Just a crossword tattooed at the top of your bum-crack
to ease the monotony

Real men play Russian Roulette with swords

I would have done it,
if he'd only asked

I can pretend,
if that's what you want

Well done,
now tell me what colour panties you've got on

I quite like my hair being pulled

I'm married but,
I would die and go to heaven if another woman licked my breasts.

Now your incontinence is funny

GO DOWN ON HER
I DOUBT YOUR DAD BOTHERS TO ANYMORE

IT WAS TOUCHING CLOTH FOR A BIT TOO,
AS I LATER FOUND OUT

WE HAVE TO AS WE DON'T HAVE A SHOWER CURTAIN

IF I'M STANDING UP IT'S EXCITING
IT MEANS I'M DOING IT SOMEWHERE I SHOULDN'T.

SHALL WE AGREE A SAFE WORD NOW OR LATER?

THINK HOW MANY WOMEN MUST BE NAKED RIGHT NOW IN THE WORLD,
IMAGINE HOW MANY HAVE THEIR HANDS IN THEIR PANTS!

THERE SHOULD BE THE SOUND OF A SWANNY WHISTLE EVERY TIME A GUY GETS AN ERECTION.
THEN WE CAN HEAR WHEN BLOKES GET A RANDOM BONER

LET'S ALTER WIKI TO SAY PEOPLE AREN'T DEAD

IF THE MEDIA GETS HOLD OF THIS, IT'LL RUIN MY CAREER

I'D LIKE TO LIVE IN THE COUNTRYSIDE
AND HEAR RUBBISH LOCAL NEWS FOR A CHANGE, INSTEAD OF KNIFINGS AND SHOOTINGS.

I'D LIKE A 'FASCINATOR' MADE FOR MY 'MAN IN A BOAT'

HOW VERY LOWEST DENOMINATION MALE OF YOU
TO ASSUME NON-PENETRATIVE SEX ISN'T SATISFYING

I'VE OFTEN THOUGHT YOU SHOULD BE ABLE TO SEE FARTS
YOU COULD THEN SEE WHERE IT DISSIPATES, AND ALSO WHO DUNNIT

I'VE GIVEN UP EXPECTING PEOPLE TO BE COMPETENT AT THEIR JOB
BUT ITS A NICE SURPRISE WHEN THEY ARE

I'M NOT SURE THERE IS SUCH A THING AS 'TOO MUCH MUSTARD'

WHAT A PAIR WE WILL MAKE.
YOU BRIGHT LIGHT WHERE ONCE WAS DARKNESS.
I BRING JOY WHERE THE SUN DOESN'T SHINE.

VALIUM AND WEED MIGHT DO IT

I REFUSE TO LET SOMEONE INSIDE UNTIL I HAVE FINISHED.

I WANT TO LIVE IN THE COUNTRY AND HAVE LIVESTOCK
NOT MORE THAN ONE OR TWO THOUGH. THINK OF THE SMELL.

I'M NOT SURE THEY WOULD CALL THEMSELVES LESBIANS.
THEY'VE ONLY HAD THE OTHER AS A GIRLFRIEND AND WOULDN'T NECESSARILY TAKE ANOTHER GIRLFRIEND

WIGGLE IT AROUND A BIT
IT MIGHT BE BECAUSE ITS SO TITCHY

I LIKE DOING LOADS OF THINGS AT ONCE
MY BRAIN LIKES EFFICIENCY. I THINK MY MUM MAY HAVE SLEPT WITH A GERMAN

I KNOW WHO THEY ARE
I JUST CHOOSE TO FORGET

AN ISLAND OF CALM IN A SEA OF NONSENSE

I LOVE THE ONE EYEBROW THING HE HAS GOING THERE

MENSA TESTS ARE EASY ENOUGH TO PASS
I JUST RESENT HAVING TO PAY TO JOIN

LIKE BOWLING BALLS IN A HAMMOCK

I'VE CAUGHT SOUTHERN.
EVERY TIME I GO HOME TO MY MUM'S I HAVE TO TURN THE HEATING ON FULL-BLAST AND COVER UP WITH CARDIES.

OH FOR GOD'S SAKE YOU BUNCH OF FUCKING SHEEP!
I HOPE YOU'RE PROUD OF WHAT YOU'VE DONE

FUCK ME LIKE YOU HATE ME

CAN'T YOU SUCCUMB TO MY CHARMS FOR ABOUT 23 SECONDS?
THAT'S ABOUT ALL I WILL NEED.

SHE LOVED HIM,
BUT HE LIKED COCK AND THEN HE DIED. THIS IS WHY SHE IS SAD

SOUNDS LIKE SOMEONE'S GOT A NASTY YEAST INFECTION

I THINK I COULD MANIPULATE HER INTO DOING ANYTHING I SAID.
THAT'S PRETTY SEXY

THEY SHOULD REPLACE EVICTION WITH EXECUTION.
AND THEY SHOULD TELEVISE THAT BIT

AM I THE ONLY PERSON IN THIS COUNTRY WHO SEES THIS GOVERNMENT FOR WHAT THEY ARE?
PARODIES OF THEMSELVES.

I SHOULD HAVE DONE MORE TODAY

THAT'S NOT DOWN TO THE BEARD THOUGH
I RECOMMEND CLOTHING

OOH, I'VE HAD THAT.
THE CONSTIPATION MAKES IT WORSE

I DON'T NORMALLY SAY THESE THINGS IN PUBLIC
I ONLY DO IT TO SHOW OFF TO YOU LOT

YOU CAN DO ALL THREE
YOU'RE A GIRL

STICK A COLD SPOON UP YOUR ARSE
AND DRINK WATER FROM THE BOTTOM OF A GLASS WHILE STANDING ON YOUR HEAD.

YOU KNOW YOU CAN'T GET PREGNANT USING THAT ORIFICE DON'T YOU?

I AM ACCIDENTALLY ON PURPOSE DRUNK.
I WISH I COULD DO THIS MORE OFTEN.

ARE YOU PROUD OF THAT?
YOU UNPLEASANT BITCH.

DON'T BE SO MEAN!
HE'S TRIED ALL THE HAEMORRHOID CREAMS HE CAN.

SHE WOULDN'T HAVE FELT IT,
EVEN IF YOU HAD A COCK THE SIZE OF THE MOON.

IT WAS LIKE WAVING A HOCKEY STICK
IN THE MIDDLE OF WEMBLEY STADIUM

HE FINISHED HIS MEAL AND WITH THE REMAINS OF IT ON HIS CHIN SAID,
"I THINK I AM READY TO SLEEP WITH YOU NOW".

I AM A CELEBRITY
AND I AM DESPISED BOTH ON AND OFF SCREEN.

I DROPPED ONE IN OLD COMPTON STREET THE OTHER EVENING
THEY ARE PROBABLY STILL TALKING ABOUT IT.

WHY AM I IMAGINING YOU
SPIT-ROASTED AND COVERED IN CHICKEN FAT RIGHT NOW?

I LIKE RUBBING THE MOUSE WHEEL ON MY LADY COCK

I'LL WAIT HERE UNTIL YOU RETURN
FINGERING MY BUMHOLE AND YELPING YOUR NAME EVERY SO OFTEN

IT'S A 'NEW AND IMPROVED' CLEAVAGE ACTUALLY
FIVE DAYS ON THE PILL SO FAR. I LIKE THIS SIDE EFFECT.

I CAN'T GET AWAY WITH SNEAKING ANY OF THEM OUT

IF YOU DON'T STOP BEING STUPID AND UNPLEASANT
I'M GOING TO GET MY DAD TO FINGER YOU

HE LAUGHED WHEN I TOLD HIM I HAD TO PUT THE FISH DOWN THE TOILET
I CRIED. I DON'T KNOW WHY I CRIED.

DID YOU GET ON TOP AND RIDE THE WAVES?

I FINALLY LEFT YOUR BUILDING AT 5.45AM
YOU MAY HAVE HEARD THE WHIPPING. WE WERE RATHER DRUNK. IT WAS FAILED WHIPPING

I LIKE HER BUT SHE HAS A SADNESS BEHIND HER EYES

IT DOESN'T MATTER WHAT YOU DRESS LIKE
WITHIN SECONDS YOU'RE DRENCHED IN FAKE BLOOD AND SEMEN AND YOU'VE BEEN MOSHED TO WITHIN SECONDS OF HAIR STYLE DEATH

NOT AFTER THE G-STRING, MARMITE AND MOTHER IN-LAW INCIDENT

I DIDN'T REALISE IT WAS YOU FROM BEHIND
UNTIL I SPOTTED THE EARS.

MOVE A LITTLE SO I CAN PEEK DOWN YOUR CLEAVAGE AGAIN

YOU HAVE LESS FACIAL HAIR THAN THE AVERAGE FEMALE

I AM ALL FOR SEX IN UNUSUAL PLACES
NO, NOT UP THE BUM, JAMES.

I THINK YOU'RE FIBBING
I MAY HAVE TO ADMINISTER A SPANKING.

I'VE JUST DISCOVERED THAT THE GIRL I LIKE ISN'T SINGLE,
AND I THREW UP ON MY TROUSERS. THESE FACTS ARE UNRELATED

I JUST LOOKED IN THE MIRROR.
I SUSPECT I MAY HAVE GINGER HAIR

HE DOES WRONG THINGS TO MY GIRL-BRAIN.
I KNOW HE'S VERY BORING IN REAL LIFE BUT HE STILL SENDS SHIVERS DOWN MY SPINE

IT'S LIKE, THREE BLOKES NOW, THAT HAVE BEEN ALL...
"I'M IN LOVE WITH YOU BUT I CAN'T BE WITH YOU BECAUSE OF ONE TORTURED MENTAL STATE OR ANOTHER"

HAS THE SCARY MAN GONE AWAY YET?

A GIRL SHOVED HER FINGER UP MY ARSE ONCE.
I WAS PLEASANTLY SURPRISED

I TEXTED MY DAD TELLING HIM I MISSED HIS THROBBING COCK IN ME
I'LL HAVE TO GET A BOYFRIEND NOT CALLED DAVE. IT'S HAPPENED BEFORE TOO.

I THINK I MAY HAVE PUT MY CONTACTS IN THE WRONG WAY ROUND TODAY
EVERYTHING IS A BIT BLURRY.

I GUESS YOU HAD TO BE THERE...
OR BETTER STILL, SOMEWHERE ELSE.

RED WINE IS GOOD FOR THE CIRCULATION.
IF I DRINK ENOUGH OF IT, I WALK ROUND IN CIRCLES.

I TOLD HIM I MUST HAVE BITTEN MYSELF IN MY SLEEP OR SOMETHING

I HAVE NEVER ONCE DIED IN AN ENCOUNTER WITH A DRAGON.
THEREFORE, I DEEM DRAGONS TO BE PERFECTLY SAFE.

HE PASSED OUT AND GAVE ME A BIT OF A FRIGHT,
BUT NOT AS MUCH AS THE EX WHO CAME ROUND, SAT BOLT UPRIGHT, AND DEMANDED LOUDLY AND ANGRILY 'WHO THE FOOK KILLED ME?'

YOU DO REALISE
THAT IF YOU SURVIVE TO THE END OF JANUARY I OWE JOHN A FIVER, DON'T YOU?

I HAD A MASSIVE TUNA BUTTY ON MY WAY TO THE POSTPONED SEMINAR.
WELL, OBVIOUSLY I DIDN'T KNOW IT WAS POSTPONED UNTIL I GOT THERE.

THE SUSPENSE MAKES ME DRINK LIKE A FISH
IF FISH DRINK THAT IS. DO THEY?

FARTING IS ONE OF THE DANGERS OF YOGA,
WITH ALL THAT STRETCHING AND FOLDING.

I WOKE UP TO FIND HIM TRYING TO PUT HIS DICK IN MY MOUTH
I ASKED HIM WHAT HE WAS DOING AND HE SAID HE WAS TRYING TO STOP ME SNORING.

YOU NEED TO GET YOUR ROOTS DONE AGAIN,
NEEDS MORE BLACK, LIKE THOSE ESSEX GIRLS

SORRY I'M LATE, I JUST FUCKED MY EX-BOYFRIEND …
… DO YOU MIND IF WE GIVE TONIGHT A MISS?

STOCKINGS ARE 'FUCK-ME SOCKS'
TO GO WITH YOUR 'FUCK-ME SHOES'.

BLIMEY! I GOT NOTICED
I THOUGHT I WAS GENERALLY IGNORED AND SMILED AT IN A POLITE 'NOW GO AWAY AND BE QUIET' KIND OF WAY.

THE BARMAID JUST ASKED ME HOW MUCH I EARN,
I DON'T KNOW WHAT'S WORSE, THE QUESTION OR THE ANSWER.

WHY DOES HE REMIND ME
OF THE CHILD CATCHER FROM CHITTY CHITTY BANG BANG?

WHAT'S THAT LONG THING BETWEEN HER LEGS?

A STRANGE SHAPE,
BUT I HAVE SEEN WORSE HERE TONIGHT.

THE MAN ASKED ME IF I WAS COMING BACK TODAY,
I SAID NO, SO HE WHEELED HIS GENERATOR IN THE SPOT AS I DROVE OUT.
I DIDN'T TELL HIM IT WASN'T MY SPACE.

I'M BREATHING FIRE FROM EVERY ORIFICE RIGHT NOW

THE BRAINS ARE ALL UNDER THE TABLE

I THINK IT WAS MORE A CASE OF WHO *DIDN'T* I FUCK AT THAT PARTY!

YOU ARE SICK.
AND I DON'T MEAN IN THE GOOD WAY.

CAN A HOLE BE A BODILY PART?
BY DEFINITION IT IS AN ORIFICE OF NOTHING.

I FIND I HAVE TO DISAGREE WITH ANYTHING
THAT WOULD SLOW DOWN MY BEER CONSUMPTION.

OR TONIGHT WE COULD CALL YOU 'BIG BIG' FOR SHORT.

NOT IN FRONT OF THE CHILDREN.

ANOTHER 'LISTENING TO THE MASSES' DECISION?
ALSO KNOWN AS 'WE DON'T KNOW WHAT WE ARE DOING, WE ARE OPEN TO
SUGGESTIONS'

I COULD NEVER UNDERSTAND
WHY MY FATHER WOULD OBSESSIVELY WATCH THE FEMALE FLOOR ROUTINES.

I KNOW WHO HE IS
I WAS BEING - OBVIOUSLY UNSUCCESSFULLY - AMUSING.

IF YOU HAVE BEER LEFT THEN THE DECISION IS MADE.
NEVER GO TO BED WITH UNFINISHED BEER, IT'S THE UNWRITTEN RULE.

WHY CAN'T THE MEDIA SAY THESE NICE THINGS ABOUT PEOPLE WHEN THEY ARE LIVING?
THEY CAN'T HEAR THEM DEAD.

I FAIL AT IRONING SO I CAN'T BE THE PERFECT WOMAN.
THEN AGAIN I'M GREAT AT GIVING ORAL SEX SO ALL THINGS EVEN OUT IN THE END.

YOU SAY YOU'RE NOT
BUT WE'VE SEEN THE VIDEO EVIDENCE TO THE CONTRARY.

EVERYONE DRAWS A COCK WHEN THEY FIRST USE A DRAWING TABLET?
I MUST HAVE MISSED THAT PAGE IN THE MANUAL.

WITH MY SVELTE FIGURE, BLONDE HAIR AND MASSIVE TITS,
GETTING MEN IS LIKE SHOOTING FISH IN A BARREL

THE BAT IS MADE FROM THE WOOD OF THE WILLOW TREE, THE BALL IS MADE OF LEATHER
I DUNNO WHAT IS INSIDE THE LEATHER BUT IT FUCKING HURTS WHEN IT HITS YOU IN THE FACE

Just because they do it in the films you watch
doesn't mean it's normal or that we actually like doing it

Good grief!
A minge with a comb-over

You won't like me when he's angry

I near choked on my Malibu when I saw it suddenly rise up!

On a video shop's shutters in Liverpool someone had written
"You fat bastard we've got your Dracula video ha ha ha". This tickled me immensely.

The last laugh was on the emu it seems.

And there's me thinking he only emptied his sack under the tree

Trust me,
there is nothing charming about mixing Y-fronts and stockings.

I wouldn't like that anywhere near my nuts!

I want mine filled please

I've had great fun and success
carrying mistletoe in my flies at a New Year's Eve party.

My mother in law is staying.
I would happily donate her services free.

When you are full of self loathing and self doubt
just tune into morning TV with your hangover and realise that life can get a fuck of a lot worse

So these hairs on my palms are OK then?

Thanks for showing it to me....
I haven't laughed this much in a long time.

My eyes have gone all kinda blurry
I don't pleasure myself so it can't be that.

That's Liverpool they steal your hub caps
Manchester they just shoot you. Get your norvern monkey stereotypes right.

I stayed in the penthouse suite
Britney Spears and Madonna slept in the same bed I slept in.
Unfortunately - not at the same time as me.

My daughter apparently shares a birthday with Hitler
She has her younger siblings salute her and goose step round the playroom

Why do you always have to come first?
It's not a fucking race!

My first thought was that he was giving birth.

YOU FOUND THE ONLY BAR IN LONDON THAT HAS NO NAME OUTSIDE
THAT YOU HAD AN IDEA VAGUELY WHICH ROAD WAS IN AND A BAR NAME YOU WOULD
HOPEFULLY REMEMBER IF YOU SAW IT. IS THERE NO WAY OF AVOIDING YOU?

THE DRUGS ARE OBVIOUSLY NO LONGER WORKING.

I'LL DO WORK FOR BEER

JUNIOR 69ERS?

I CAN STAY AT HOME AND BE INSULTED BY AN EXPERT

TWO PINTS FOR A POUND?
MAKES LIVERPOOL ALMOST SOUND ENTICING. ALMOST.

IT MAKES PERFECT SENSE IN AN IMPERFECT WORLD!

I HAVE A SAW AND A POWER DRILL WITH ATTACHMENTS.
YOUR WISH COULD BE MY COMMAND.

TYPING 'PENIS'
IS SO MUCH LESS TIRING ON THE FINGERS THAN 'PURPLE HEADED WOMB BROOM'

NOT AS AWFUL AS MINE
MINE ARE FAMOUS FOR THEIR AWFULNESS.

I HATE IT WHEN I BURST OUT LAUGHING, AND I CAN'T EXPLAIN WHY.

WHAT'S WRONG WITH TWO NUBILE YOUNG WENCHES FROM TRANSYLVANIA SHOWING THEIR ARSES?
WORKS FOR ME. WHO CARES WHAT THEY SANG.

ANYWHERE ELSE THAN HERE
AND THAT WOULD HAVE MADE HEADLINE NEWS

I ONCE WOKE UP NEXT TO SOMETHING THAT LOOKED LIKE THAT.
I'VE CUT DOWN ON THE ALCOHOL SINCE THAT DAY.

THAT ONE LOOKS A BIT FAULTY.
HAVE YOU BLOWN IT UP INSIDE OUT?

IT'S MINE, I'LL WASH IT AS QUICK AS I LIKE.

IT WAS NEVER LIKE THAT IN MY DAY
WHEN TREES WERE REAL AND CARS RAN ON LEAD AND RUBBER BANDS.

WAS THAT SEEN THROUGH BEER GOGGLES?

I SMELL LIKE A LESBIAN'S ROLL-UPS THIS MORNING.

THE REAL TURNING POINT
IS WHEN YOU FIND YOUR MAN BREASTS ARE BIGGER THAN THE GIRLFRIEND'S.

THINK HOW DEEP THE SEA WOULD BE IF IT WASN'T FULL OF SPONGES.

I THINK HE HEARD
BUT HE NO UNDERSTAND

WE ARE STILL NONE THE WISER
BUT WE ARE CONSIDERABLY OLDER

BELIEVE IT OR NOT, I SAID THAT AT A MEAL OUT WITH FRIENDS. TWICE.
THEN FELT REALLY STUPID. THEN FELT I NEEDED TO GET AWAY FROM THERE.

SHE GAVE YOU WHAT?
SORRY, I SHOULD HAVE SAID THAT MORE QUIETLY.

I DIDN'T CALL YOU A C**T.
IT WAS THAT C**T OVER THERE. YOU C**T.

AT 1:17AM
WHO GIVES A FLYING FUCK

YOU THINK TOO MUCH..
IT'S NOT GOOD FOR YOU, AND EVEN WORSE FOR US.

LOSES SOME OF IT'S ENIGMATISISM.
IS THAT A WORD?

IF I HAVE EGGS ANYWHERE NEAR MY BREAKFAST TABLE,
THEY HAD BETTER BE UNFERTILISED.

I DON'T THINK HE CLAIMED RESPONSIBILITY FOR HER ACTIONS.

WAY TO GO: 10% TALENT, 80% OPTIMISM, 20% PRESCRIPTION DRUGS.

WAS HE THE ONE WHO PISSED IN THE BIN?

NOTHING THRILLS ME MORE
Than sleeping with a married man and pretending I'm his wife.

MY WIFE SPEAKS FLUENT RUSSIAN
Was it swear words you were after? Most people are.

I SMOKED LAST NIGHT
As I always seem to do after five pints.

I DROPPED MY SANDWICH IN MY GLASS OF SCOTCH
Improving the taste of one immeasurably, but sadly marring the other

I BOW TO YOUR SUPERIOR KNOWLEDGE OF THREESOMES

HANGOVERS COMPLIMENT THE FUN TIMES LEADING UP TO THEM
Enjoy them. If not for them every arse would be out drinking

HE AND HIS WIFE HAVE FULLY INTERCHANGEABLE PARTS.

OH... DID I SAY THAT OUT LOUD?

IT ALSO TRIGGERED THE SECURITY LIGHTS
Which meant I was spotlit, todger out, sprawled over a child's pedal car.

OOPS. SORRY IT'S SO BIG

I WANT A DOUBLE OF WHATEVER YOU'VE BEEN ON.
And I need it right now!

I HATE FRENCH CHAMPAGNE
ANYONE WOULD THINK THEY INVENTED IT THE WAY THEY GO ON ABOUT IT.

I SWEAR AMERICAN GIRLS TAKE ORAL SEX LESSON'S AT SCHOOL
AND THEN MAJOR IN IT AT UNIVERSITY. IT SEEMED THAT WAY AT THE ONE I WENT TO.

HOW CAN YOU BE SO UGLY WITH ONLY ONE HEAD?

THEY PAID FOR A PRIVATE LAP DANCE FOR ME
COMPLETELY STARKERS. PISSFLAPS TO THE WIND!

THE ONLY THING GOOD TO COME OUT OF FRANCE WAS THE CHANNEL TUNNEL.
OH, AND THE WINE. AND THE PERFUME.
AND THOSE FUNNY LITTLE WHITE FLUFFY SWEETS.
AND THE OCCASIONAL CHEESE.
AND THE HORSES. - NO MAYBE THEY DON'T COME OUT OF FRANCE.
AND THE VIADUCTS...

YOU'RE RIGHT. I DIDN'T LAUGH

MY FATHER BROKE THE NEWS BY SAYING "FLOPPSY'S A GONNA"
"YOU CAN HAVE STEW AFTER ALL."

ONLY THE NOSE, THE SCARY PART IS THE REST IS ALL REAL

HE'S NOT THE NUTTER.
IT'S THE PEOPLE WHO BELIEVE WHAT HE SAYS IS 100% TRUE.

I HAD TO WATCH IT A FEW TIMES TO TAKE IN ALL THE SUBTITLES.

Is that the gusset of a pair of pants?

If he could breathe through his ears he would be perfect

I'd tried to tell her the size didn't matter,
but deep down I could tell she was disappointed.
- With my effort for the village fete, I mean.

Tonight I'll make you forget all about your horrible day.
I won't tell you how, but you will forget.

Always admit to unintentional brilliance.
I do. Or just smile knowingly and let them think you knew all along.

You'd think they could find a stripper
without bingo wings for goodness sake!

As opposed...
to an unreal live one?

I think I'll join you in that.
Let me know when we start shouting "Jerry! Jerry! Jerry!"

I didn't get it either
but I didn't want to be the one who admitted it.
Now I can blame you and sit here smugly pretending I did.

And then everyone copies that tripe for years afterwards.
Fascinating world.

HE WOULDN'T DO THAT - NOT UNLESS SHE HAD A COCK.

MEGA FOREHEAD
HE WAS BORN PHOTOSHOPPED.

I NEVER USED TO LIKE ANAL,
BUT NOW I DON'T FEEL LIKE I'VE BEEN PROPERLY SHAGGED UNLESS I'VE DONE IT

SOD BATTLESHIPS!
I'LL BE PLAYING 'SINK THE SAUSAGE' WITH A FEW YOUNG EASTERN EUROPEAN GIRLS.

THE NURSE IS GOING TO CHECK MY PROSTATE NEXT WEEK
I'M REALLY LOOKING FORWARD TO IT

I'VE GOT A FRIEND DOES THAT FOR ME

THAT IS AN IMAGE I COULD DO WITHOUT THIS MORNING.

THE ONLY TAKE-AWAY YOU DON'T HAVE TO CARRY HOME.
YOU JUST SAY 'WALKIES'

YES, NOW YOU'VE FINISHED YOUR SNIGGERING,
YOU CAN TELL ME WHERE YOU GOT THAT PICTURE OF MY PENIS!

IT'S NOT THE SIZE THAT MATTERS, HUN,
WELL ACTUALLY, I TELL A LIE...

I LIKE THAT
MAYBE JESSICA RABBIT WOULD BE GOOD IN THAT FANTASY TOO.

She must have had plenty of sevensomes then

Was he was using a Dick Van Dyke Cockney accent?

She looks strangely human in that pic.
A first for her.

I wanted to credit you, but I couldn't remember your name

Surely she'd notice it running down her thighs.

There is no such thing as a bad blow job.

I strongly hope that is only a list of notes to yourself

Porn is what God made Google for

It's all to be found in Brownian's motion.
His first of the morning usually.

Damn,
I got found out.

Did you mean to say that out loud?

But... did he inhale?

I ASKED HIM IF HE WANTED TO BACK TO MY PLACE.
HE SAID WOULD HOLD OUT AND SEE IF HE GOT A BETTER OFFER.

TALKING OF HAND ACTION...

HANG ON TO YOUR DRINKS
SHE'S JUST PUNCHED THE WRONG GUY.

I LEFT 20 QUID ON HER BEDSIDE TABLE
NOW SHE CAN'T DECIDE WHETHER TO TELL ME OFF FOR TREATING HER LIKE A WHORE, OR FOR VALUING HER PERFORMANCE SO LOW. I'M NOT SURE WHETHER TO TELL HER IT WAS SO SHE COULD CATCH A TAXI TO WORK OR JUST WATCH HER ANGER.

SHE MAY HAVE BEEN TOTTY ONCE
BUT I AM GUESSING A GOOD 20 YEARS AGO.

THE FRENCH INVENTED PERFUME - THEY HAD TO!

BACK IN THE DAYS OF THE RAJ,
WE WOULD MAKE OUR EXCURSIONS INTO THE BUSH IN THE DAYS BEFORE LADIES TRIMMED THEM, AND I WOULD BE CONFRONTED BY A PAIR OF GIIIIINORMOUS... WHAT WERE THEY CALLED... TEETH, THAT'S IT.
BLOODY BUGGERS, I SHOT THEM RIGHT BETWEEN THE SEAMS AND I'D BE ORF BEFORE YOU COULD SAY "PULL YOUR TROUSERS UP YOU FILTHY SWINE" BUT I DIGRESS.

AT THE RISK OF APPEARING STUPID,
WHAT IS HE HOLDING IN HIS HANDS?

CAN YOU BE A BIT GAY?

Let's smear ourselves in Swarfega
and play naked twister

I love my MSN ignore button
I will be campaigning for one that works in real life at the next election.
Any party that can provide one gets my vote.

I saw it.
How did you know my name was Hardly Anyone?

The other day was sooooo yesterday,
don't you think?

Let her stew,
Get out your old porn collection and remember the good times when women were free and easy

It would never win,
unless there was some nudity, deformity, sick animals or transvestisism

Serious haircut,
when you walk out without a body

You'll get no sympathy here
unless you pay in beer and sexual favours.

All we need now is
John Inman in those ridiculous lederhosen shorts from 'Are You Being Served'.

NEVER MIND THE QUALITY
FEEL THE GIRTH

IT WAS SOME EASTERN BLOCK OLYMPIC TEAM,
NOT PORN THIS TIME

WHEN HE ANNOYS ME
I USE HIS TOOTHBRUSH TO CLEAN THE TOILET.

IS THAT A POLITE WAY OF SAYING
TAX COLLECTOR?

I REALISED IT PROBABLY WASN'T THAT CLEVER,
EVEN AFTER SERIOUS QUANTITIES OF SINGLE MALT SCOTCH.

SHE IS ONLY KNEE HIGH
YOU CAN TAKE HER HOME IN YOUR POCKET.

THEY CALLED IT 'MY DEEP FRIED LAUNDERETTE'
IN SCOTLAND

IT'S BOUND TO HAVE TOM CRUISE
AND BE A PILE OF HOLLYWOOD SHIT.

I BET THE PRACTICALS WERE FUN TO WATCH

MAYBE YOU COULD ALSO TRY UNDER 'SERVICES'.
OR MASSAGE.
OR HAND JOB.

Why can I never drink enough?

What is the purpose of them?
They don't make you bigger or last longer.

I'm not keen on people who make me waste beer by spilling it.

Unless you stuck it up a cows arse

I show respect for age
I enjoy old scotch and young women.

I have recommended him to some very unsavoury sites
He will not be able to sleep for a week.

Clutching and straws spring to mind.

A bit crawly bum lick,
but don't stop.

'Boutique beer' sounds a bit gay

It's been fifteen minutes since the last one,
I was getting desperate

And so you should be.
Doing that with lunch time approaching.

I BET THE OOMPA LOOMPAS HAD BETTER LUMPAS ON THEM.

I AM GONNA USE THAT ALL WEEK -
'A BIT DEVELOPMENTAL' FOR ANYTHING CHAOTIC.

WHEN YOU HAVEN'T TAKEN ANY, AND YOU SEE ELEPHANT FACES,
THAT IS THE TIME TO START WORRYING.

A GOLF BAG FULL OF PENCILS IS RELEVANT?

I BET THE SWEDISH VERSION WAS BETTER

HE MAY FIND A WOMEN WITH BETTER BOOBS
AND A MOUTH LIKE A DYSON

ISN'T IT ONE OF THOSE THINGS PEOPLE WITHOUT HANDS USE TO PAINT?

THIS WEATHER MAKES MY HUSBAND CHECK OUT LADY BULGES
I REALLY DON'T MIND BUT I WISH HE'D NOT SLOW DOWN SO MUCH TO DO IT.

MORE FUN THAN A MOUSE ON A STICK

I REALISED I COULD FOR THE FIRST TIME IN MY LIFE CLASSIFY MYSELF AS 'NORMAL'.
EVERYONE ELSE WAS EVEN WEIRDER THAN ME.

THAT IS JUST SICK!

It may be the age old pint and a kebab for a fumble in the knickers,
or the more expensive purchase of earrings for a quick back-scuttle, but it always comes down to finances in the end.

They probably bounce well though

It will corrupt you.
It did me.

I didn't want to suffer alone with that image in my head.

Her face looks like it's melting wax

Did she gargle?

I give up
Who are you?

Fine pair

Prod it hard and see what happens.

I've been waiting for everyone to go out
so I can try it.

No one came back on your 'semi' then?

WHAT IS WORRYING IS THAT YOU HAD THAT PAIR OF LUCKY PANTS THEN, AND YOU STILL HAVE THEM NOW!

A LOT OF PENT UP FRUSTRATION ABROAD TODAY

IT IS FAR HARDER TO MAKE SOMETHING SOUND WRONG AND AMUSING THAN IT IS TO MAKE IT SOUND RIGHT. AND YES I'VE SEEN X-FACTOR.

IT ALSO SHAVES HER LEGS.
QUITE A FEAT

IT'S JUST ONE OF THOSE DAYS
I HAVE ALL THE GOOD IDEAS. EVERYONE ELSE HAS THE ANGER.

THE DEVIL WILL BE KISSING HIS ASS.

SHE'S OPEN TO OFFERS.
TO A NAME THAT IS.

IT DEPENDS WHERE HE WENT.
IF IT WAS ONE OF THOSE GOLFING HOLIDAYS IN THE CARIBBEAN THAT HAVE TOPLESS CADDIES AND BILL HIGH CLASS HOOKERS AS 'ROOM EXTRAS' THEN SHE SHOULD BE UPSET.

HOLD TIGHT.
WE'RE OFF.

YOU CAN SPOT THEM BY THEIR SIZE, THEIR SHIFTY EYES, AND THE DRIED SEMEN STAINS ON THEIR TROUSERS.
THE BOYS LOOK NORMAL THOUGH

THAT AWFUL FEELING
WHEN YOU REALISE YOU'VE JUST VOMITTED YOUR WAY OUT OF PROBABLY YOUR ONLY EVER CHANCE OF A TEENAGE THREESOME.

A PAPER CUT THERE DOES SOUND PAINFUL, I AGREE.
THOUGH I AM CURIOUS WHAT YOU WOULD BE DOING IN THE OFFICE WITH YOUR KNOB OUT

THE JUDGE WIPED AWAY HER TEARS WITH MY FUCKING CHEQUE BOOK

SOMETIMES I LIKE TO USE MY LEFT HAND
AND PRETEND IT IS SOMEONE ELSE.

I THINK I'VE SLEPT WITH EVERY GUY IN HERE UNDER 30 ALREADY.

A WOMAN IS COMING ROUND TO QUOTE US AN EXTORTIONATE AMOUNT FOR TABLE DECORATIONS AND A BALLOON ARCH AT OUR WEDDING.

I AM HERE ON A COMPUTER DATE, BUT THE COMPUTER DIDN'T TURN UP

THE WAITING AND EXPECTATION IS THE BEST PART,
AND NOT KNOWING WHETHER YOU'RE GOING TO GET ANYTHING.

WANKING DOES NOT MAKE YOU VOTE CONSERVATIVE.
IT MAY HELP THOUGH.

I CAN'T REACH THE BRAKES ON THIS PIANO!

MORE LIKE A FIT THAN DANCING.

YOU'LL ONLY FEEL A LITTLE PRICK.

DON'T LOOK.
I DID AND MAY NEVER BE THE SAME AGAIN.

WHY, OH WHY, DID YOU HAVE TO ASK?

I HAVE TO WASH THE GUILT FROM MY THIGHS.

I HAD ONE TEACHER BOUNCE A WOODEN BLACKBOARD DUSTER OFF MY HEAD.
DIDN'T DO ME ANY HARM. I WAS COMPLETELY MAD BEFORE THOUGH.

DOES SHE COME WITH A HEALTH WARNING STAMPED ON HER ARSE?

I PUT UP WITH HIS LIES AND CHEATING
BECAUSE THE SEX IS SOOOOO DAMN GOOD.

'CHAP STICK'
WAS NOT ONE OF THE POSSIBLE ANSWERS I HAD IMAGINED.

I GAVE MY BIKE UP,
THE GRAVEL DISAGREED WITH MY SKIN.

I KNOW WHAT YOU ARE TALKING ABOUT
BUT I DON'T WORK OPPOSITE ANYONE.

SHE'S MADE OF PLASTIC AND SILICON
AND OPERATED BY STRINGS.

YOU'D BE SURPRISED WHAT SOME OF THE STUDENTS
OFFER ME IN RETURN FOR GOOD GRADES. SO WOULD MY WIFE.

I SHAGGED HER ON THE CONFERENCE TABLE
YOU CAN STILL SEE THE MARKS.

THAT'S GOOD,
FROM A LOT OF ANGLES.

IF A POLICE OFFICER TOLD ME TO GET OUT THE CAR AND SPREAD 'EM
I WOULD, IN A SECOND.

I HANG OUT WITH RICH PEOPLE
THAT WAY I GET LAID BY ASSOCIATION.

IT'S ONLY A PROBLEM
WHEN YOU READ OUT LOUD WHILE TYPING.

I READ 'SHAVING AGAINST THE GRAIN' AS 'GROIN'
WHICH SURPRISED THE AUDIENCE..

I RECORD MY NEIGHBOURS HAVING NOISY SEX
AND POST IT ON THE INTERNET.

I THINK SHE COMPLIMENTS IT

A TRUE GENIUS COULD NOT GIVE BIRTH TO A 'NORMAL' CHILD,
AS SHE SO PROVES.

I KNOW AN EX OF HERS
AND FROM WHAT HE SAYS, YOU DEFINITELY SHOULD.

MY GRANDMOTHER THOUGHT THE INTERNET
WAS THE WEBBING FOUND INSIDE SWIMMING TRUNKS

I FOUND A WEDDING RING IN MY BED LAST NIGHT.
I'M NOT MARRIED.

EVERYBODY SHUT UP.
SHUT UP. THIS SONG IS ALL ABOUT ME.

HE PUT ON THREE STONE TAKING MIRTAZAPINE FOR FOUR MONTHS.
THEY MUST HAVE BEEN FUCKING BIG TABLETS

THAT'S THREE BEERS
AND A BIG WET GIRLY KISS ON THE BOTTOM YOU OWE ME NOW

THERE GOES THE POOR GUY'S MASTURBATORY FANTASY

I HAD A THOUGHT THE OTHER DAY
ALL MPs ARE WANNABE ROCK STARS OR TV STARS THAT WERE JUST TOO UGLY TO MAKE IT.
YOU LOOK AT MPs. ONE STEP AWAY FROM CRIMEWATCH PHOTOFITS MOST OF THEM

I WISH I HADN'T APOLOGISED FOR PISSING IN THE SINK IN HER ROOM
SHE'S JUST TOLD ME SHE DOESN'T HAVE A SINK IN HER ROOM.

FORESKIN DORK TECHNIQUE

NOTHING INSPIRES MY CREATIVITY LIKE AN IMPOSSIBLE DEADLINE

HAVE YOU SEEN MATRON ABOUT THAT PROBLEM?

WHEN I CAME HOME EARLY
HE WAS WEARING MY BRA AND PANTIES!

YOUR NAME SUGGESTED TO ME YOU WERE MALE.
I AM AFRAID THE IMAGE IN MY HEAD WHEN YOU SPOKE ON THE PHONE WAS NOT GOOD.

A FEMALE OF THE CLOTH IN STOCKINGS AND SUSPENDERS?
THAT COSTS DOUBLE ROUND MY WAY

I FOUND AN OLD VAUXHALL CAVALIER ON EBAY
DESCRIBED AS 'SUITABLE FOR RAM RAIDING'.

WE OPENED THE ADVENT CALENDARS THIS MORNING.
MY 2 YEAR OLD DAUGHTER COULDN'T UNDERSTAND WHY WE OPENED ONLY ONE WINDOW WHEN THERE WERE ANOTHER 24 STUFFED WITH CHOCCIES. HOW DO YOU ARGUE WITH LOGIC LIKE THAT?

THAT MAKES ME A LOT DISTURBED.
MAKE IT STOP.

GO BUY SOME DONUTS
I WANT TO EAT THEM FROM YOUR DICK.

WHAT IS A BOOGER?

Painful in the way that whenever I hear him singing
I can only think his trousers were much too tight or his nuts were in a vice.

He's getting reflective.
Must mean the bottle's now empty and reality is kicking in

It's all blurred without my glasses
All I can guess is that it is Miss Piggy bending over.

My parents told me I was allergic to ice cream when I was little.
So I never noticed ice cream vans after that. Funny how many things I was allergic to when I was little I was suddenly 'cured' of when I grew up.

He tried to make me wear women's clothing.

Anyone can write.
What we want is blood, sweat and tears.

Holy snappin' arseholes, Batman

Thank you all for shouting at me earlier.
You made me feel loved again in a strange way.

Ties can be interesting.
But probably only in bondage

Half the world's population is Chinese
which makes my sister Chinese I believe

SHE CAN HEAR A CHOCOLATE WRAPPER TWO MILES AWAY

MISS WORLD CONTEST IS ON TV
NO WONDER IT IS QUIET IN HERE AND THERE IS A NATIONAL SHORTAGE OF KLEENEX.

I GUESS THAT ONE WILL NEVER SLIP OFF YOUR LAP

AS A LOWLY STUDENT LIVING IN A SQUAT IN SOUTH LONDON
A HEAD POPPED UP AT MY WINDOW ONE DAY AND ASKED IF I WANTED TO SELL MY OLD VICTORIAN FIREPLACE.
IT WAS ROLF HARRIS. I SAID NO AS IT WAS MY ONLY FORM OF HEAT.
LATER THAT DAY UPON RETURNING TO MY ROOM, MY FIREPLACE WAS MISSING.
I LATER FOUND OUT THE GUY UPSTAIRS HAD TAKEN IT. I DON'T KNOW WHETHER HE SOLD IT TO ROLF, BUT FOR AGES I THOUGHT ROLF HAD STOLEN MY FIREPLACE.

I'VE JUST HAD A FACIAL.
WHY ARE YOU ALL LAUGHING, IS THERE SOMETHING ON MY FACE?

MEN DO NOT NOTICE SKIN BLEMISHES AND UNUSUAL ANGLES,
WE JUST PICTURE YOU BENT OVER BEING ROUGHLY TAKEN

NSFW STANDS FOR 'NOT SAFE FOR WORK' NOT 'WIFE', YOU DORK!

I ALWAYS SUSPECTED HE HAD ANAL INCLINATIONS

I ACCIDENTLY TYPO'D THE SCRIPT.
AT REHEARSALS I WAS TAKEN BY SURPRISE WHEN HE SAID 'WANK THE PLANK'.

I STOOD AT THE BACK OF THE ROOM.
IT LOOKS WORSE FROM THERE.

I HAVE ANNOYED YOU?
THEN MY EFFORTS WERE NOT IN VAIN.

BUT...
CAN HE BREATHE THROUGH HIS EARS?

I'D FORGIVE YOU FOR BEING BORED,
BUT HORNY IS UNFORGIVABLE

AND THEY CAN FLY BACKWARDS?

YOU SEARCHED FOR 'CLITTY'?
AND YOU GOT JAPANESE PHOTO BOOTHS?

EVERY TIME I LOOK AT HIM
I WORRY HE IS GOING TO SET HIS WHISKERS ON FIRE.

I HOPE THAT CAKE WASN'T EXPENSIVE.
IT LOOKS CRAP.

ISN'T SHE THE ONE WHO PUT THE WINE BOTTLE UP HERSELF?

WHEN YOU SUDDENLY REMEMBER IT'S YOUR WIFE'S BIRTHDAY
AND YOU HAVE NO PRESENT TO GIVE HER. THAT IS KNOWING REAL FEAR

BLIND PEOPLE ARE FUN
ESPECIALLY WHEN YOU MOVE FURNITURE IN THE ROOM WITHOUT TELLING THEM.

THE LIPS BULGE THE OPPOSITE WAY.

I KNOW A BLOKE IN A NATTY HAT THAT CAN FIX ANYTHING.
THE BLOKE, NOT THE HAT.

THEY ARE INCREDIBLY DIFFICULT TO PLAY.
HAVE YOU MASTERED YOURS?

HOW MUCH THEY CAN REMEMBER
DEPENDS ON HOW CLOSE TO CLOSING TIME IT IS.

IT'S EITHER AN X-RAY OF A HEART OR A DISTORTED LADY PART,
DEPENDING ON HOW YOUR MIND WORKS.

THEY WERE SAGGY AND FLAT TO START WITH THOUGH.

WHY? WHY? WHY? DO I CLICK ON THOSE LINKS?

ALL THESE YEARS I HAD BEEN PUTTING IT ON MY GENTLEMAN'S AREA
SILLY ME.

HOW MANY POTATOES DID THEY HAVE TO PAY HER?

YES DEAR, IT WAS THE BEST 30 SECONDS OF SEX IN MY LIFE

CAUGHT THE LAST TRAIN HOME.
SUDDENLY WOKE UP AT MY STATION IN A PANIC AND JUMPED OFF THE TRAIN.
AS THE TRAIN PULLED OUT I REALIZED I'D ONLY GONE ONE STOP AND HAD TO WAIT
SIX HOURS ON A COLD MISERABLE PLATFORM TILL THE FIRST TRAIN NEXT MORNING. I
WOULDN'T HAVE MINDED IF I'D GONE ALL THE WAY TO THE END OF THE LINE. AT
LEAST I WOULD HAVE GOT SOME SLEEP AND FEEL I'D ACHIEVED SOMETHING IN THE
WAY OF TRAVEL AND EXPLORATION.

I TRY TO START A NEW RELATIONSHIP BEFORE ENDING THE LAST ONE
IN CASE IT DOESN'T WORK OUT

MEN ARE THE HARD POINTY ONES
WOMEN ARE THE SOFT LUMPY ONES

IF SHE WAS A MILIONAIRESS, NYMPHOMANIAC, HEIRESS TO A BREWERY
WHO OWNED THE WORLDS FINEST COLLECTION OF BENTLEYS AND ASTON MARTINS I
WOULDN'T CARE WHAT SHE LOOKED LIKE. BUT SINCE SHE'S NOT...

ALWAYS DICED CARROTS AND TOMATO SKINS
BUT I NEVER REMEMEBER EATING THEM

I CAN'T FIGURE OUT IF SHE IS RIGHT
OR I'VE HAD TOO MUCH TO DRINK.

THE DRUNK WHO GETS A LAUGH FIRST TIME,
THEN INSISTS ON RETELLING THE JOKE IN MORE DRAWN OUT DETAIL OVER AND OVER.
AND THEN GETTING NO MORE LAUGHS SAYS IT MUCH LOUDER

PERHAPS THIS IS RAW EDGE
CUNNINGLY DISGUISED AS CRAP

I REFUSE TO CLICK ON ANY MORE LINKS.
I HAVE HAD SOME TRAUMATIC EXPERIENCES TODAY.

LATELY I HAVE BEEN TRYING THE 90 SECOND SHAG BREAK FROM WORK.
MY SECRETARY DOESN'T SEEM TO APPRECIATE IT AS MUCH AS I DO, BUT I DO
REMOVE ALL THE SHARP OBJECTS FROM THE DESK BEFORE HAND.

VERY FASHIONABLE ON BRITISH BEACHES
ALONG WITH THE KNOTTED HANKY ON THE HEAD

BRILLIANT VALENTINE'S DAY GIFT FOR AN EX.

IF THEY GROW UP STILL LOOKING LIKE HIM
THAT'S WHEN YOU NEED TO WORRY.

FOR ONE AWFUL MOMENT
I THOUGHT THAT WAS A TOILET BOWL

THE SURPRISE WOULD NOT BE PROJECTILE VOMITING BY ANY CHANCE?
AFTER ALL THAT SPINNING.

I ONCE WOKE UP NEXT TO SOMETHING LIKE THAT
SOMEONE MUST HAVE SWAPPED HER FOR THE ONE I STARTED WITH DURING MY DRUNKEN SLEEP.

I'M A ROCK STAR. LET'S TRASH YOUR HOTEL ROOM.
IT'S EXPECTED.

THAT SHOULD COME WITH SOME KIND OF WARNING ATTACHED.

READING ABOUT THEM,
IS AS CLOSE TO MEETING SOME OF THEM AS I WOULD SAFELY LIKE TO GET

THE BIGGEST SURPRISE IS NOT HOW FAT THEY ARE,
BUT HOW TINY THEY ARE. MOST FIT IN YOUR POCKET.

MAYBE SHE VOMITED HER WAY SLIM AGAIN

THAT LOOKS SUSPICIOUSLY LIKE SOMETHING MY WIFE OWNS
WHICH BUZZES.

IS THIS THE RIGHT ROOM FOR AN ARGUMENT?

IF YOU LIKE HIPS WITH A SHIT LOAD OF FAT HANGING OFF THEM.

DOES 'ARYAN' MEAN WOMEN WHO LOOK LIKE BUTCH BULL-DYKES?

MORONS WHO FORGET THE RADIO MIC IS STILL LIVE.
GOING TO THE TOILET IS COMMON PLACE, BUT A MARRIED NEWSREADER TRYING TO
GET A SHAG OFF ANYONE WHO IS AROUND IS GOOD BLACKMAIL MATERIAL.

THE MAJORITY OF PEOPLE AROUND THE WORLD ALL WANT THE SAME;
PEACE, HARMONY, GOOD SHAG, AND TO BE HOSPITABLE.
THIS APPLIES TO EVERY COUNTRY EXCEPT THE FRENCH.

THAT MAKES ME WRIGGLE IN MY SEAT

MY GIRL WANTS TO JOIN IN

I FIND CHAMPAGNE HELPS BETTER.

IF YOU WEREN'T HERE
I WOULD SAY WHAT I REALLY THINK

DO YOU MAKE A HABIT OF SMELLING MUSICIANS?

WHAT IN DARNATION WAS HE DOING WITH THAT HAND?

WHOOSH
THE SOUND OF ANOTHER MISSED DEADLINE.

YOURS LOOK LESS STREAMLINED.
LESS POINTY, BUT STILL GOOD.

A TYPICAL NIGHT OUT IN ZOMBIEVILLE

THAT'S THE NICEST THING ANYONE HAS SAID ABOUT MY WORK.
IT'S THE ONLY NICE THING ANYONE HAS EVER SAID TOO, SO TRY TO START A TREND.

IT'S NOT SO BAD
BUT I HAD TO YOU USE ALOE VERA AFTERWARDS.

I LOVE VODKA STRAIGHT
SO JUST SPIT IT THIS WAY RIGHT OUT THE BOTTLE

THE SICK PART OF THE IDEA WAS ALL MINE.

FROM A MALE POINT OF VIEW
I THOUGHT THIS APPROPRIATE.

YOU LOOK LIKE A DOG IN A BOBBLE HAT.

HAVE YOU BEEN REPEATEDLY PESTERED
BY A MAN WITH A NECK-BEARD AND A GARY NEVILLE SHIRT AS WELL?

I SPEAK FLUENT DRUNKEESE.
IT COMES IN USEFUL. I'VE WON SOME FISH AND A FEW ODD FRIENDS ON THE STREETS OF SOHO IN THE PAST.

MAKE IT BIGGER!

THAT'S ABSOLUTE BOLLOCKS!
NOW REARRANGE THOSE WORDS UNTIL THEY ACTUALLY MEAN SOMETHING

THAT REALLY LOOKS LIKE A CHEW THING MY DOG HAS.

I THINK IT'S THE WEATHER.
OR THE GOVERNMENT.
OR THE TRANSPORT INFRASTRUCTURE.
OR OUR SHIT CRICKET TEAM.
DAMN, I AM WHINGEING NOW.

ANYONE CAN BUY FLOWERS AND CHOCOLATES.
TROUBLE IS WOMEN THINK DIFFERENTLY TO MEN. YOU NEVER KNOW WHAT IS RIGHT TILL IT'S TOO LATE.

THAT IS DISTURBING
IN SO MANY WAYS

YOU ARE RIGHT. IF YOU BLINK AT THE RIGHT RATE IT DOES.

NICE SCARS.

And I thought I was the only one who liked that film.
The rubber gloves scene still makes me giggle like a girl.

I believe there is a strong element of 'The Emperor's New Clothes' about the place.
If Tracey puts a bed in there it's art. If I put a bed in there I get asked to leave.

I only drew the knob
The rest was already there

I'm constantly washing my hands
And worrying about getting herpes from glasses in restaurants.

I have been screamed at for something 100 times less offensive.
Depends on the time of the lunar cycle.

The Australian barman whinged on and on
About how us pommies whinge all the time.

Is it safe to put in my mouth?

It's my ex, The Wicked Witch of the West, I think

Wear your sweatshirt backwards when on a session
Then you can throw up in the hood.

You made me spit on my keyboard

I THINK I MAY BE WEARING MY PANTS BACKWARDS
I couldn't find an opening in the gents.

BLOODY TOURISTS
It's not lie-ses-ter square, it's **LEICESTER** Square.

WHENEVER I SEE A COUPLE TOGETHER
I imagine what type of sex they have. I've imagined you, and you are filthy.

WE WILL NEVER TELL.
EVER.
EXCEPT FOR MONEY

TWELVE POUNDS?
For that you get free insults thrown in as well.

IS 'PISSTAKES' ALL ONE WORD?

THE WALL BARS IN THE DISABLED BOG ARE THERE FOR ONE REASON-
to sink your teeth into after a particularly evil curry.

YOU COOKED IT WITH IT'S HAT ON?

I LOVE THE COMFORTING FEELING OF DEPRESSION.

WHY ARE YOU STILL HERE?
Take her home she's ready!

NO FUN WHEN STUCK BETWEEN YOUR TEETH

I'VE NEVER PEE'D ON A GIRL. AT LEAST NOT WHILE SHE WAS AWAKE.

I SAW IT IN A SHOP. IT WAS FOR YOUNG GIRLS.
WELL THE SHOP WAS NOT FOR YOUNG GIRLS.
THE FILM WAS.
I HAD BEST SHUT UP

A WHOLE BOTTLE OF BAILEY'S?
HOW CAN ANYONE DRINK A **WHOLE** BOTTLE?
STAND BY WITH A BUCKET.

I HAVE FOUND MYSELF HOLDING MANY A GIRL'S HAIR BACK AND SAYING,
'OF COURSE I WON'T TELL ANYONE IN THE MORNING'

IT'S DEBBIE DOES **DALLAS**
NOT DERBY!

I CAN RELATE TO THAT,
HAVING A 21 MONTH OLD THAT SECRETES FLUIDS FROM EVERY ORIFICE.

IT'S THE **ORGASMATRON** FROM BARBARELLA.
GIVES ORGASMS. DOES WHAT IT SAYS ON THE TIN.

NOT MY TASTE BUT, HEY, SOMEONE MUST LIKE IT THAT WAY.

DAMN, HE COULD HAVE SOMEONE'S EYE OUT WITH THAT!

THE TYPE NOT EVEN A MOTHER COULD LOVE.

TOUGH CROWD IN TONIGHT

DON'T LET THEM GET YOU DOWN
I HAVE HAD ABUSE HURLED AT ME FOR YEARS.

IF HE WANTS TO.
LET HIM.

I WENT TO ROME
I NEVER MET THE POPE ONCE.

SIXTY-FIVE TITS?
STOP. THE IMAGES HURT, ESPECIALLY THE THOUGHT OF WHY THE ODD NUMBER.

MAYBE HE'S TRYING FOR THE SATURDAY NIGHT PITY SHAG.

I THINK IT WAS A DAMN GOOD EFFORT
CONSIDERING HOW QUICK YOU WERE

ANYTHING WITH TITS IS ALWAYS POPULAR AROUND PUB CLOSING TIME

THAT'S WHY THE END OF THE DICK IS LARGER
TO STOP YOUR HAND SLIPPING OFF AND PUNCHING YOU IN THE EYE.

MAYBE IT'S A DYSLEXIC IN-JOKE

HE SAID DISCUSS
NOT WRITE A BLOODY ESSAY

I BET YOU ARE FUN AT PARTIES

ESPECIALLY AFTER TEN PINTS,
AS I HAVE FOUND THE NEXT MORNING

IF I HAD EDITED THE GRAMMAR AND CORRECTED THE SPELLING,
IT WOULD HAVE MADE NO SENSE.

HOW COME YOUR FRIEND HAS A PICTURE OF ME
IN STOCKINGS ON HIS PHONE?

THE HUMPTY DUMPTY SYNDROME
ONLY WAY TO CHECK IF IT BOUNCES IS TO DROP IT

WHEN YOU GET HOME A SCHOOLGIRL WILL BE WAITING
IN FRONT OF THE FIRE WITH A WARM HEART AND NO PANTIES, FOR HER SPANKING
AND WARM CREAM.
I HASTEN TO ADD THAT TEXT WAS FROM MY WIFE AND NOT A GENUINE SCHOOLGIRL

I LEAVE A PAIR OF STOCKINGS AT THE END OF MY BED EVERY XMAS
I AM NOT ABOUT TO STOP NOW.

DON'T LOOK NOW BUT THAT BITCH IS IN HEAT,
I SAID DON'T LOOK NOW.

YOU ARE NOT YOUNGER THAN YOU LOOK.

DON'T TRY TO DENY IT,
YOU ARE ALMOST WORLD FAMOUS

I HAVE THIS HORRIBLE SUSPICION
THAT WHEN IT LIFTS ITS DRESS, IT HAS A BIGGER PENIS THAN I DO.

AND THE ROOM SPINNING...
THAT'S THE ...(THROWS UP)

WOULD YOU RATHER I HAD SAID, "MY GOD IT'S FULL OF COCK"?

I CAN'T PUT MY FINGER ON WHY.
NOR WOULD I WANT TO.

WHEN I AM IN GERMANY I JUST SAY 'BEER'.
WORKS EVERYWHERE FOR ME.

IF SHE DOESN'T ANSWER
GIVE HER ONE.

HIGHLY SPRUNG

I WISH I'D MARRIED MY WIFE'S SISTER
NOW I KNOW SHE'S BETTER IN BED.

I AM ASSUMING YOUR QUESTION WAS IRONIC.

'BEER PANCAKES' WINS MY VOTE

EXECUTIVE INCLUDES EVERYTHING MASSAGED, AND SOME EXTRAS.
OR SO I AM TOLD.

IF I'D HAVE KNOWN THAT BEFORE,
I'D HAVE PUT CLEAN UNDERWEAR ON.

IT IS A SOCIAL FAUX PAS
ARRANGING YOUR SOCIAL LIFE SO FAR IN ADVANCE

NO WAY DO I WANT THAT ADDRESS SITTING IN MY HISTORY PAGE

DID HE JUST SAY
'WHILE OUT PLANE SPOTTING'?

THEY ARE HYPNOTICAL.

ONE WOMAN AT A TIME IS JUST NOT ENOUGH

ISN'T ONE OF HER SON'S GAY?
I SHOULD BE CAREFUL, IT MAY STILL BE TREASON TO SAY IT.

AFTER SEEING THAT
I AM NOT HOLDING ANYONE'S HAND

ISN'T HE THE GUY FROM THAT PROGRAM?

HAVE ANOSSSER DRINK, GOOO ON.
HIC

STOP CHUCKIN' THEM BLOODY SPEARS
YOU'LL 'AVE SOMEONE'S EYE OUT

I TOLD MY HUSBAND I WAS A LESBIAN SO HE WOULD DIVORCE ME
HE WANTS ME EVEN MORE NOW.

A HAND JOB WOULD BE WELCOME I ASSUME?

BEFORE I COULD SAY I'M NOT THAT KIND OF GIRL, I WAS.

I CAN BURP-TALK
BUT THE BOYFRIEND ISN'T VERY GOOD AT IT.
BURP TALKING THAT IS.

PLUCKING IS PAINFUL.

THAT EXPLAINS WHY MY MOTHER IS SUCH A FAN OF HIS BOOKS
THE DIRTY COW.

STOP TEXTING ME, I'M SITTING RIGHT NEXT TO YOU!

HE WASN'T ACTUALLY IN ME
BUT TELLING HIM? – EMBARRASSING OR WHAT?

I SOBERLY GIVE YOU PERMISSION TO DO THAT TO ME DRUNK LATER.

DID I JUST SAY COCKS INSTEAD OF CLOCKS?

IT WAS SO FAST I MISSED IT
BUT HE SEEMED PLEASED WITH HIMSELF

MOST WELCOME ON A SUNDAY MORNING,
OR ANY MORNING IN FACT.

HER THIGHS CHAFF AS SHE WALKS

I CLIMBED OUT THE WINDOW WHEN HIS MUM CAME HOME,
SHE NOW THINKS HE MOANS HIS OWN NAME IN A GIRLY VOICE WHILE WANKING.

SOME THOUGHT HAS GONE INTO IT
RATHER THAN JUST PAINTING SOMETHING GREEN AND PUTTING A FRAME AROUND IT.

HER BOYFRIEND AND HER DIGNITY ARE BOTH OUT OF TOWN TONIGHT.

I THOUGHT IT ENDED WITH 'SOMEONE WIPE THEM OFF'?

I TOUCHED MYSELF IN CHURCH.

I'VE ALWAYS SAID THEY WERE THE SAME PERSON

I TRIED TO THINK OF GENTLY ROLLING GREEN HILLS...
BUT ALL I COULD SEE WERE ROUNDED BUTTOCKS AND WARTS IN THE VALLEYS

DID HE SAY WHAT I THINK HE SAID?

IS THAT A ONE LEGGED PERSON REFLECTED IN THE SIDE WINDOW?

HE THINKS I AM ON THE PILL.

PERHAPS WINNING EVERYTHING GOES TO SHOW
HOW MUCH CRAP THERE IS TO COMPARE IT TO.

TALKING OF SMALL...

REALLY?
THAT MAKES MY LOCAL DAIRY A MAMMAL.

STUDDED ANTIQUE LEATHER SHOULD BE SAT ON,
NOT WORN.

I DON'T CARE WHAT THEY SOUND LIKE, I WOULD.
TOGETHER.

THAT HAS GOT TO BE A BIG ONE

A DICK IS A DETECTIVE.
IT IS, ISN'T IT?

DID YOU IMAGINE HER FROM BEHIND?
I KNOW I DID.

WHAT YOU LACK IN HAIR
YOU MAKE UP FOR IN NOSE.

I WOULD LIKE TO COMPLAIN ABOUT THIS IN THE STRONGEST TERMS
I AM NOW GOING TO WRITE A STERN LETTER TO THE DAILY MOAN.

IS THAT A SHADOW OF FEAR I SEE?

THERE YOU GO BRINGING BALLS UP AGAIN.

YOU BASTARD
I CAN SMELL THAT FROM HERE

I TOOK MY KIDS TO THE LEGO SHOP IN BLUEWATER
NO, THEY DON'T BUY THEM. I WANTED TO BUY SOME LEGO.

CAN YOU COME WITH ME?
WHEN I AM OUT WITH YOU PEOPLE TELL ME I HAVE LOST WEIGHT.

JUST AS WELL IT'S NOT GIN
THERE WOULD BE NO HOLDING YOU BACK.

CAN NATURE TRULY BE THAT CRUEL?

IT'S THE TONGUE IN THE CHEEK, COCK-SUCKER ACTION

EVERYONE TELLS HIM IT IS
BUT HE SAYS IT'S THE ONLY DRINK THAT DOESN'T HURT HIS TEETH

BY THE TIME I FOUND OUT IT WAS TOO LATE,
SO I THOUGHT FUCK IT, A BLOW JOB'S A BLOW JOB.

GIVING UP IS EASY, I HAVE DONE IT LOADS OF TIMES

I CAN'T COPE WITH TALKING TO YOU IN BOTH PLACES AT ONCE

FUCK OFF BACK WHERE YOU CAME FROM,
AND TAKE YOUR FERRET WITH YOU.

IT SEEMS TO BE FIGHT NIGHT,
WHO AM I TO STAND IN THE WAY OF A DAMN GOOD ARGUMENT?

IT SAYS EIGHT OUT OF TEN WOMEN USE SEX TO GET MALES TO DO THEIR BIDDING.
THE OTHER TWO MUST BE TOO UGLY.

I'VE HEARD HIM CALLED A LOT OF THINGS
BUT LITTLE WAS NOT ONE OF THEM.

IT'S MY BIRTHDAY NEXT WEEK
I'M SCARED MY BOYFRIEND WILL FIND OUT HOW OLD I REALLY AM.

DO IT THEN
AS I HAVE NO IDEA WHAT YOU MEAN.

I FOUND OUT MY GIRLFRIEND MASTURBATES TO LESBIAN PORN.
AT LAST I'VE FOUND SOMETHING WE HAVE IN COMMON.

I GET THE IMPRESSION
YOU WERE A TINY BIT ANGRY WHEN YOU WROTE IT

HER HUSBAND IS SIXTY YEARS OLD
BUT THEN AGAIN, HE CAN AFFORD TO TRADE HER IN FOR AN EVEN YOUNGER MODEL.

JUST CLICK ON RANDOM JAPANESE WORDS AND SEE WHAT HAPPENS.

WHAT'S 'TEABAGGING'?

SHE SOUNDS READY, GET HER ROUND, VIDEO HER.

THE WAY THEY MOVE INDEPENDENTLY OF EACH OTHER IS DISTURBING ME.

THOSE WHO MAKE MOST NOISE OFTEN HAVE LEAST TALENT.
I FOR ONE AM GUILTY OF BEING NOISY.

DISHONOURABLE DISCHARGE?
THAT'S SOMETHING I USED TO FIND ON MY PYJAMAS IN THE MORNING.

POSSIBLY
BUT I DIDN'T SWALLOW

SOMEONE TOLD ME PRINCESS DIANA IS DEAD
PRINCESSES DON'T DIE. THEY JUST FALL ASLEEP FOR 20 YEARS.

NEVER OVERESTIMATE THE INTELLIGENCE OF THE AVERAGE WORKER

THOUSANDS OF 'EM,
SWARMING IN LIKE FLIES ON A BUTTERED BUM.

TOO MUCH ROUGE AND TOO LITTLE CLOTHES,
A SURE SIGN OF DESPERATION IN A WOMAN.

THAT'S A DEFINITE TWELVE PINTER

THAT RULES OUT ORAL AND BUMSEX TOO.
POOR CATHOLICS.

I AM ADDICTED TO ADDICTIONS
IF A NEW ONE COMES ALONG, I JUST HAVE TO TRY GETTING ADDICTED TO IT.

THERE WERE POSH TARTS SPOTTED IN LONDON.
I THOUGHT THEY HAD BEEN HUNTED TO EXTINCTION.

SPEED KILLS!
CAREFUL HOW MUCH YOU TAKE

MARRIAGE DIDN'T STOP ME WANTING TO FUCK EVERY WOMAN I SEE.

THE DRUNK TRAIN HOME
WOULD PASS THROUGH, PURLEY, PURLEY OAKS, PURLEY SOUTH, PURLEY NORTH - I ALWAYS WONDERED IF ONE DAY IT WOULD SURPRISE ME AND STOP AT PURLEY GATES.

THAT'S PUT ME RIGHT OFF THE SCOTCH EGG I WAS CONTEMPLATING

I AM NOT SURE I LOVE YOU ENOUGH TO LEAVE MY HUSBAND.
HOW MUCH ARE YOU WORTH?

DOES THAT MEAN YOU STOLE IT?

AND THAT'S MEG. OTHERWISE KNOWN AS BOB FOR SHORT.

USE ONE OF THOSE NEW FANGLED COMPUTER THINGAMIES

Time has not been kind to her,
and her knees are now as big as babies heads.

My wife wants to know why I came home from a gay bar
with condoms in my pocket. Which one of you bastards is the joker?

And missed the chance of annoying so many people?
With my reputation?

Those wrinkled stockings he wore last time
are still seared into my memory.

Happy birthday.
Open the booze

I get it, we think of a word and then add it in our mind?
It's true art for the beholder.

Quite incredible pelvic action

I saw him live at a small stand-up venue.
I went for a pee and there was the man himself taking a piss.
I of course chose the adjacent urinal and annoyed him by talking to him
and looking at his cock. – He isn't funny off stage.

How long you got?
My list is embarrassingly long.

I'd go for baldy if anyone cares

THE HOTEL STAFF WERE NONE TO PLEASED WITH YOU.
YOU DRANK THE WATER FROM A FLOWER VASE AND THEN ASKED FOR ANOTHER "ONE OF THEM BIG MARGARITAS".

NO GENTLEMAN WOULD ADMIT TO COMING FROM WIGAN.

HE HAS A TOUCH OF THE ROBERT ROBINSONS ABOUT HIM

YOU PUT FAR LESS WORK IN THAT THAN MEETS THE EYE.

I WAS KINDER TO MY DOG THAN MY GRANDMOTHER
SHE WAS FORCED TO SUFFER FOR TWO YEARS.

DON'T LISTEN TO THE BUGGER
SHE'LL FIND OUT EVENTUALLY.

MADE ME LAUGH MORE THAN YOUR GRANNY WOULD FIND ACCEPTABLE
PLEASE OFFER HER MY APOLOGIES AND A LARGE BOTTLE OF GIN.

IT DEFLECTS YOUR THOUGHTS AWAY FROM THE CRAPNESS OF THE FOOD

GOSH,
SOMEONE EVEN MADDER THAN ME

WHAT DO YOU MEAN BY 'GETTING FISTED'?

YOU'LL NEVER KNOW HOW GOOD WE COULD HAVE BEEN TOGETHER
I'LL MAKE SURE NO ONE ELSE DOES EITHER.

Did you ladder your tights on the desk?
Our old receptionist was always moaning about her ladders and trying to show anyone who was brave enough to look.

I woke up in a strange bed
and a strange kid who spoke some foreign language crawled in beside me and called me papa.

It's a full moon
Don't try to understand anything from now on.

I want to see a picture of the bitch
you think worth ruining our relationship for!

That woman just crawled under the table.

I went to a modelling call today.
It said "no experience necessary" but then they wanted to know why the hell I didn't bring any professionally-taken photographs

I am leading him on.
He's falling in love with me, when he does I'll break his heart.

That was World War One
Only they couldn't call it 'One' until the kick-off whistle for 'Two' had been blown.

An inflatable arse?
How rare.

I'VE NEVER BEEN 'TROUTED' BEFORE.
DO I HAVE TO BEND OVER?

SIMPLE AND EFFECTIVE.
LIKE ME

VERY GOOD FOR YOU PERHAPS
NOT FOR ME

I OPENED TWO BOTTLES OF BEER
DEJA BREW?

I THOUGHT TO MYSELF...
THAT'S ONE WEIRD SCROTUM

WHAT'S A NICE GIRL LIKE YOU DOING IN A SHITHOLE LIKE THIS?

THAT'S A HE, SURELY?
YOU CAN TELL BY THE HAT

IN REPLY TO THE QUESTION YOU ASKED YESTERDAY.
THE ANSWER IS STILL NO

I ENJOY SHARING MY WORK WITH OTHER PEOPLE
WHETHER THEY LIKE IT OR NOT.

I LOVE YOUR LIPS.
THEY'D LOOK GREAT WRAPPED ROUND MY COCK.

YES I'VE FAKED AN ORGASM WITH YOU,
EVERY FUCKING ONE!

SHALL WE PUT IT IN THE FRONT OR THE BACK?

THE IRONY IS PAINFUL
BUT OH SO TRUE.

DARK MY ARSE!
THE FACT IT WASN'T MY BED SHOULD HAVE BEEN A BIG ENOUGH CLUE!

HAND OUT THE FLUFFY PILLS

THAT'S EITHER GENUINE
OR SOMEONE HAD A LOT OF TIME ON THEIR HANDS

I REALISED THAT I HAD STORED IT UNKNOWINGLY ALL THESE YEARS
AND THEN SPAT IT OUT IN A PIECE OF WORK I THOUGHT WAS ORIGINAL.
I AM NOT ACCUSING YOU OF BEING UNORIGINAL THOUGH.

MY DAPPY GREAT-AUNT TURNED UP EARLY FOR MY BROTHER'S WEDDING.
ONLY SHE THOUGHT SHE WAS LATE. THE COUPLE GETTING MARRIED BEFORE NOW
HAVE PICTURES OF A STRANGE OLD LADY THEY DON'T KNOW.

I FEEL LIKE A LESBIAN TRAPPED IN A MAN'S BODY.

I READ OUT ROUGE AS 'FUDGE' ON THE 6PM NEWS BROADCAST.

WORKING OUT LIMB OWNERSHIP IS MAKING MY EYES GO WEAK

JUST SHOUT IF YOU NEED ME.
UNLESS YOU ARE STANDING NEXT TO ME OF COURSE.

DRESS REALLY TARTY SO HE KNOWS YOU MEAN BUSINESS.

ALL THE 'GOOD AND PROPER' ENGLISH LADIES I KNOW
SWEAR LIKE TROOPERS AFTER A GLASS OR FIVE OF BUBBLY.
IT'S ALL THAT 'GOOD AND PROPER' CONVENT SCHOOL EDUCATION

SURELY 'YES' IS NOT AN OPTION TO STATUS.
MARRIED, DIVORCED, SEPARATED, AND SINGLE WOULD BE OPTIONS.

FOR ONE AWFUL MOMENT THERE
I THOUGHT YOU SAID YOU WERE LOOKING FOR TRANSVESTITES.
HANG ON... YOU DID, DIDN'T YOU?

DOUBLE THE IRONY
IS NOT PRESSING TWO PAIRS OF JEANS.

SOMETIMES THE SLIGHTEST HINT OF A NIPPLE
AND YOU GET HAULED OVER THE COALS - OR AT LEAST I DO

SHE WAS NOT AT ALL LADYLIKE.
DOWNSTAIRS I MEAN.

THIS IS A COMMON OCCURRENCE DOWN MY LOCAL RUGBY CLUB.
SO THERE WAS ME THINKING IT WAS NORMAL BEHAVIOUR.

DO I NEED TO BE YOUR BITCH?

WHY DOES MY PISS SMELL OF SUGAR PUFFS?

I COULD SAY YES....
BUT I WOULD BE LYING

I JUST PRAY HE REMEMBERS TO TAKE HIS MEDICATION REGULARLY

SKEETING IS WHAT THEY DO IN NEWCASTLE ON ICE.

THERE I WAS RETURNING HOME TO OLD BLIGHTY,
DONE BATTLE WITH THE OLD HUN, LEAD GONE FROM MY PENCIL, NOTHING ON THE
CLOCK BUT THE MAKERS NAME, MORE HOLES THAN A BRADFORD BROTHEL IN THE
KITE. NOTHING LEFT FOR IT BUT TO BROLLY-HOP INTO THE BRINY AND FLAG DOWN A
PASSING JOLLY JACK TAR.

DON'T 'E SOUND POSH WHEN 'E SAYS "BOLLOCKS".

IT IS WARMED BETWEEN THE THIGHS OF YOUNG MAIDENS
BEFORE BEING IMBIBED INTO THE CUP TO ADD TO THE FLAVOUR, IF THAT HELPS.

I SLIPPED ONE TO THE NEW TEMP. SEC. AT WORK
THE ONE WITH THE LEGS THAT GO ON AND ON TILL THEY REACH HEAVEN.
A SAUSAGE IN THE BACK PASSAGE ROUND BY THE BIKE SHEDS.
IT WAS A BIT MUDDY, BUT I THINK NO ONE NOTICED.

MUCHO POLITICAL UNCORRECTNESS. I LOVE IT.

I ROLLED MY EYES AT HIM,
AND HE NEVER ROLLED THEM BACK TO ME.

THINGS HAPPEN. SOMETIMES DISTURBING, OTHER TIMES ILLEGAL, BUT ALWAYS THINGS. AND YES, YOU CAN BRING WOMEN

I HAD SOME UNEMPLOYED, ILLEGAL, FOREIGN TYPES STEAL MY APPLE LAPTOP
THEY ARE LIKE MAGPIES, DRAWN TO IT'S SHINYNESS.

THAT'S GOT TO SMART.

HER FACE DOES NOT LINE UP WITH HER MOUTH.

A BAG OF CONKERS AND A BOTTLE OF SCOTCH AS PAYMENT

BRILLIANT
AND AT A SPEED I CAN COPE WITH.

NANNY SAYS IT IS NOT GOOD FOR MY EYESIGHT TO DO THIS SO LATE.

I HAVE AN EIGHT WEEK OLD BABY.
BEST CONTRACEPTIVE EVER!

MY YOU DO LIVE A COLOURFUL LIFE.
I HAVE NEVER SEEN A ROMANIAN BUTTOCK CLEFT PERFORMANCE IN MY LIFE, SO I SADLY HAVE NOTHING TO BASE A COMPARISON ON.

SOMETIMES I SHOULD JUST KEEP QUIET

IT'S UNNERVING ME.
HIS FEET POINT ONE WAY, HIS HEAD THE OTHER.

SHE SHAGGED HIM BEHIND YOUR BACK ON A TRIP TO LONDON DUNGEONS?
DIDN'T ANYONE COMPLAIN?

SO I TOLD HIM
I'M NOT A BLOODY HOBBY HORSE

IF IT'S ANY HELP
I HAVE NEVER HEARD OF 'FIST OF FUN', SO NO AMOUNT OF CLUES WILL HELP ME.

ANY PORT IN A STORM

I FEAR YOU MAY NEED TO SEEK HELP WITH YOUR MIND.

BLAME THE ALCOHOL
THAT'S WHAT I DO - EVEN WHEN I'M SOBER

I HAVE TO RUSH OFF, SO IT'S A REAL QUICKIE

TYING ME UP AND DOING ANYTHING YOU LIKE
DOES NOT INCLUDE GOING DOWN THE PUB WITH YOUR FUCKING MATES!

I HAVE HAPPY MEMORIES OF SEVENTEEN
THE AGE I GOT AN INCREDIBLY FAST MOTORCYCLE AND EVEN FASTER WOMEN

EVERY PAGE SAYS, 'MESSAGE TO FOLLOW'

YOU FORGOT TO ADD 'VOMIT' TO THE END OF THE LIST

THAT'S WHAT MY WIFE SAYS...
...HAVE YOU BEEN SEEING MY WIFE?

YOU PEAKED TOO SOON

I'D GET THAT SEEN TO IF I WERE YOU

TOILET SEATS OR UNFORTUNATE CONTACT WITH DOOR HANDLES?
NOW I CAN UNDERSTAND PRIVATE PARTS COMING INTO CONTACT WITH TOILET SEATS, BUT DOOR HANDLES BEGGARS BELIEF.

THIS CANNOT BE SEEN ENOUGH
I DROP MY KNIFE ON THE FLOOR AND SHE BENDS OVER AND PICKS IT UP.

SHAGGING HER MATE IS PROBABLY NOT THE SURPRISE SHE HAD IN MIND.

THERE AGAIN, TO BE SPOILED FOR CHOICE IS A GOOD THING.

IF THEY VOTE FOR HIM AS THEIR MP,
THEY ARE NOT PEOPLE I WANT TO LIVE CLOSE TOO.

HE THINKS BEFORE HE SPEAKS?
THAT MAKES IT EVEN WORSE.

GOD MUST REALLY HATE YOUR PART OF THE WORLD.

IT'S A BRAVE MAN THAT TAKES A WOMAN SHOPPING

I THOUGHT SEXUAL RELATIONS WERE FAMILY MEMBERS.

THAT'S WOMEN FOR YOU
*They take the real amount of lovers and divide by ten.
When I married my wife she claimed to have only slept with one-point-two men before me. That's when I first got suspicious.*

I SLEPT WITH HER ONCE
Once was enough.

MINIMALIST AND DARK
Just the way I like my women.

I WOKE UP AND THERE WAS MONEY TUCKED IN MY KNICKERS
What the hell did I get up to?

I'M WEARING THE SAME SKIRT AS YESTERDAY
It used to mean I'd been up to no good, but sadly it now means I need to do my laundry.

SILLY
But in a good bad way.

HE SAYS HE DOESN'T LOVE ME.
I won't stop following him and calling him until he realises he does.

DOES SEX EVER GET PAST THE FUMBLING AND AWKWARDNESS STAGE?
Or does school yard angst stay with us for ever?

SORRY, I COULDN'T HELP MYSELF

I MAY GET INTO TROUBLE OVER THIS
BUT IT'S NOT AS IF HE CAN SEE WHAT I AM DOING

I'VE SEEN HIM BOUNCING OFF THE WALLS
WALKING DOWN DEAN STREET. DON'T SEE HIM ON TV ANYMORE THOUGH.

THEN LATER WHEN YOU ARE ON YOUR FIFTEENTH HALF PINT
YOU WILL BUM EVERYTHING IN SIGHT INCLUDING THE PUB DOG AND THE GARDENER WHO
CAME BACK FOR THE GLOVES HE HAD FORGOTTEN AND WHO YOU SURPRISED IN THE
DARKNESS UP THE BACK PASSAGE.

JUST HAD A NIPPER MESELF, GUVNOR.
CAN'T 'MEMBER THE LAST NIGHT I GOT ANY SLEEP.

IF I WANT TO GET WRECKED
I JUST DRINK MORE OF THE STUFF THAT IS WEAKER BUT TASTES NICE

IT'S OK. I ALWAYS GET SHOUTED AT.
I'LL JUST LEAVE SHALL I?

LATERAL THINKING.
JUST ADD A PINCH OF SALT.

THE QUALITY OF THE MUSIC IS ALMOST EXACTLY INVERSE
TO HOW MANY DOLLARS IT RAKES IN.

LET ME GUESS...
TO WASTE OUR TIME?
TO DRAW ATTENTION TO YOURSELF?

I RIDE THE DRUNK TRAIN HOME AND RING UP EVERY GIRL I KNOW.
THEY HATE ME AND LOVE ME FOR IT ALL AT THE SAME TIME.

I ONCE WOKE UP NEXT TO HER.
NO IDEA HOW I GOT THERE. STILL HAUNTS ME

IS IT CHEATIN'
IF 'E WANKS AN' COMES OVER ME TITS?

TRAMPLED UNDERFOOT BY LOCAL GIRLS OF FINE DISREPUTE.
ONLY THE FINEST

MY GIRLFRIEND WATCHED THE ATHLETICS
AND STARTED WEARING SKIN TIGHT LYCRA. LIFE DOESN'T GET ANY BETTER.

IT'S MORNINGS LIKE THIS THAT MAKE GLOBAL WARMING WORTHWHILE.
I'M GOING TO LEAVE MY CAR RUNNING ALL DAY AND DO MY BIT TO HELP.

THOSE WITH LEAST TALENT SEEM TO BE THE MOST OBNOXIOUS

I SUGGEST COPIOUS AMOUNTS OF ALCOHOL,
AND A RUB DOWN BY A CHEAP WHORE WITH A DAMP CHAMMY AND REPEAT THREE
TIMES A DAY AFTER MEALS. THE EFFECTS WILL SOON WEAR OFF.

YOU SHOULD BE A POLITICIAN WITH YOUR CREATIVE USE OF STATISTICS

THAT IS JUST SO, SO, SO, SO ,WRONG!
BUT BLOODY CLEVER.

I AM GENERALLY MISUNDERSTOOD.
WHAT I DO IS EITHER TOO CLEVER, TOO STUPID, OR JUST PLAIN ILLEGAL.

IT TOOK ME AGES TO TURN IT THAT WAY.
THE ASSUMPTION WAS THAT NO ONE HAS ANY IDEA WHICH WAY UP IT SHOULD GO.

I HAVE A FRIEND THAT BUYS IT AND JUST SUCKS IT OUT OF THE TUBE.
IT MAKES ME SHUDDER WHEN SHE DOES.

QUICK, THERE'S A WISHING STAR
MAKE A WISH. AND MAKE IT FILTHY.

BOING! (SHOUTED LOUDLY IN THE MIDDLE OF A BAR FOR NO APPARENT REASON)

IT'S TAKEN SEVENTY YEARS AND GOD KNOWS HOW MUCH MONEY TO COME UP WITH AN ANSWER I COULD HAVE TOLD THEM IN FIVE MINUTES.
STUPID PEOPLE ARE HAPPIER. NOW WHERE'S MY RESEARCH GRANT? EH?

WE ALL KNEW AND LOVED THAT FUTON
OH THE TALES THAT FUTON COULD TELL... COULD PROBABLY BE READ IN THE STAINS.

HER HAIR WAS SO SOFT, TRULY LIKE SILK, I SWEAR.
DOWN TO HER WAIST, AND IT SMELLED JUST LIKE GARDENIA.

SEX SELLS APPARENTLY.
WOULD YOU LIKE TO BUY ANY?.

AN OUBLIETTE IS A HAT YOU CAN KEEP CAKE IN.

A GOOD BED IS INDEED HARD TO FIND.
I'LL JUST SETTLE FOR MY OWN AGAIN TONIGHT SHALL I?

DRINKING ESTABLISHMENTS ARE THE ONLY PLACE TO BE FRIDAY NIGHTS.
IT'S WHAT SOHO WAS MADE FOR. ONE BIG PARTY AND THEN THE DRUNK TRAIN HOME.

TEN INCH MEAT,
AND ALONE IN LONDON.

I STILL STRONGLY SUGGEST YOU GET PROFESSIONAL HELP,
EVEN THOUGH THE SAMARITANS HUNG UP ON YOU.

BUT I LIKE PEEKING THROUGH MY NEIGHBOURS BATHROOM WINDOW
YOU WOULD TAKE THAT ONE PIECE OF HOPE IN MY OTHERWISE EMPTY WORLD OF
DESPAIR AWAY FROM ME?

TRIM, DON'T SHAVE
OR YOU'LL SCRATCH HER CHIN

IT DIDN'T SAY WHETHER THE OPENING WAS HIS MOUTH OR HIS ARSE.

A PERSON'S NAME HAS A BIG LETTER AT THE BEGINNING.

A DRUNKEN MOMENT OF MADNESS IN A PUB
AND I AGREED TO PLAY RHYTHM GUITAR FOR A BAND — MOSTLY 3-CHORD PUNKY
HEAVY ROCK STUFF THAT WAS EASY TO BLUFF.
THE BAND HAD A MASSIVE FIGHT WITH EACH OTHER. 'ARTISTIC' DIFFERENCES THEY
CALLED IT. ENDED UP WITH THE DRUMMER BREAKING HIS THUMB AND THE LEAD
SINGER HAVING A CHAIR BROKEN OVER HIS HEAD. OH WELL. ROCK AND ROLL.

IT'S NOT THAT LONG
EVEN BY GAY STANDARDS.

I PAINT BETTER PICTURES WHEN I'M DRUNK.
BUT I TEND TO PUT TOO MANY BREASTS IN THEM.

MAY I BE SO BOLD AS TO ENQUIRE,
WHO THE FUCK YOU ARE?

YOU CAN NEVER BE TOO CAREFUL.
ESPECIALLY AROUND THE GENTS CONVENIENCE.

I HAD NO IDEA IT COULD LOOK LIKE THAT.

THE STUDIO CALLED A TAXI AND TOLD HIM HE HAD TO LEAVE.
HE GOT ARSEY AT HAVING TO WAIT AND KICKED THE DOOR OPEN, FALLING DOWN THE
STEPS INTO THE ROAD AND GOT HIT BY THE TAXI THAT HAD COME TO PICK HIM UP.
NOW THAT IS IRONY.

I HAVE TRIED TO AVOID PREGNANCY ALL MY LIFE
SO FAR SO GOOD.

ALL BRITS HAVE BAD TEETH.
IT'S SOMETHING WE INHERIT AT BIRTH

I'VE CHANGED SINCE LAST NIGHT, I FEEL LIKE A DIFFERENT PERSON.
AND I HAVE TROUBLE SITTING DOWN.

YOU HAVE TO CATCH YOUR FOOD BEFORE YOU CAN EAT IT.
BUT NEVER TRY CATCHING ANYTHING HEAVIER THAN YOURSELF

YOU'D KNOW IF IT WAS CLOSE TO YOU,
YOU'D HAVE TO DUCK

IT DOESN'T MATTER WHAT INNOCENT WORD I GOOGLE FOR
I ALWAYS END UP WITH SPREAD LEGS AND A DICK LIKE A DONKEY'S

IT'S BECAUSE PEOPLE SMELLED BAD IN THE OLD DAYS
BEFORE 'CHANNEL' FIVE

I'D LIKE TO WATCH ANOTHER MAN SUCK OFF MY BOYFRIEND.

IS IT DRIPPING?
THAT'S SO UNHYGENIC

TWO BLOODY MARY'S AND A POPE-ON-THE-ROCKS SHOULD DO IT.
FOR EACH OF US, I MEAN. YOU BUYING.

YOU WERE THE ONE WHO TOOK MY VIRGINITY.
TAKE IT AGAIN. IT'S BEEN SO LONG IT'S GROWN BACK.

I TOLD HER SHE LOOKED HOT AND SHE LOOKED REALLY PLEASED.
I HADN'T THE HEART TO TELL HER I MEANT SHE WAS SWEATING A LOT.

IT'S NO GOOD IF IT'S FLOPPY.

NORKS ALWAYS WIN MY FAVOUR

THERE WAS ONCE A TIME
WHEN I WAS EXCITED AT THE THOUGHT OF GETTING HOME.

I SIT ON THE FENCE.
NOT LITERALLY YOU NONCY ARSED FAIRY

BEHAVE!

I LOVE YOUR ACCENT.
NOW SAY "VODKA MARTINI, MR. BOND. SHAKEN, NOT STIRRED"

A DAMN FINE SHAG IF EVER I SAW ONE

WHY DO OLD PEOPLE ONLY LIKE OLD MUSIC?

SERIOUSLY HUNG-OVER I MISTOOK LAXATIVES FOR ASPIRIN
SPENT ALL DAY IN BATHROOM MOANING ABOUT HOW SHIT ASPIRINS ARE.

SO IT'S METAL WITH ALL THE METAL REMOVED THEN?

IT POURS DOWN EVERY TIME I GET THE LAWN MOWER OUT
I AM NOW SURROUNDED BY JUNGLE AND KNOWN LOCALLY AS A RAIN GOD.

I WOKE UP THE BABY WITH THAT.

I GET MOTION SICKNESS LOOKING AT HER

MY BOYFRIEND IS MORE IN CONTROL OF MY LIFE THAN I AM.

AND UNLESS I SEE THE COLOUR OF YOUR FIVE POUND NOTE...
THE PICS GET UPLOADED

A MILLION MILES FROM WHAT I HAD IMAGINED THEY'D LOOK LIKE.

DON'T FORGET THE KLEENEX.

I'M GETTING SICK OF ALL THE COMPLIMENTS.
SO I'VE DECIDED TO BE JEALOUS, AND HATE HER INSTEAD.

FARMYARD OLYMPICS
SOUNDS LIKE A DUBIOUS CONTINENTAL PORN FILM

LADIES CAN BE GAY

I'D LIKE A STIFF ONE PLEASE.

YOU WILL NEVER KNOW HOW MUCH THANKS YOU OWE ME

BLINDNESS IS NOT SELECTIVE OF WHAT YOU SEE IS IT?

THE DOG WAS CHEWING IT EARLIER
IT'S ONLY MILDLY DEFORMED.

SO WRONG IN SO MANY WAYS.
PERFECT.

OHHH, I KNOW!
A BUTT PLUG

I'VE CHEATED ON ALL MY HUSBANDS.

I LIKE SEX, DRUGS AND ROCK 'N' ROLL
BUT SOMETIMES LIFE GETS IN THE WAY.

JUST TELL YOUR BOSS HIS WIFE IS GOOD IN BED,
DESPITE WHAT THE OTHER STAFF SAY. THAT SHOULD DO THE TRICK.

THAT MAKES MY EYES WATER

YOU'RE NOT DEPRAVED ENOUGH FOR ME

THE ONLY THING WORSE THAN BEING DRUNK IS NOT BEING DRUNK.

FUCK RELATIONSHIPS
I JUST WANT SEX.

AS LONG AS HER FEET REACH THE GROUND WHEN SHE PEES

DON'T YOU DARE TELL MY WIFE THAT

THE WONDERFUL PSYCHOLOGY EXAMPLE IS -
YOU WOULDN'T INSULT A TABLE FOR VERY LONG AS YOU'D GET NO REACTION.

JUMPERS FOR GOAL POSTS
KICKING A ROLLED UP NEWSPAPER IN THE STREET
GYM SLIPS AND NAVY BLUE KNICKERS....
...I'LL BE BACK IN A MOMENT

GIVE A WOMAN GIFTS AND SHE'LL BEHAVE HOW YOU LIKE,
BUT GIVE HER CHAMPAGNE AND SHE'LL MISBEHAVE HOWEVER YOU LIKE.

I CHEAT WITH UGLY WOMEN.
SHE DOESN'T BELIEVE I'D DO THEM AND THEY ARE BETTER SHAGS THAN HER.

BELGIUM SMELLS OF COWS

MY WIFE INVENTED ANTI-GRAVITY.
SHE SAYS THE EXTRA 2LBS WAS BINGE DRINKING 2 DAYS BEFORE. SO FOR 2 DAYS IT WEIGHED NOTHING? NOTHING TO DO WITH THE CHOCOLATE SHE STUFFED LAST NIGHT.

THERE'LL BE BLOODY EASTER EGGS IN THE SHOPS SOON

THE DIFFERENCE BETWEEN PINK AND PURPLE IS THE SQUEEZE

COLD WATER AND BIGGER
SOMEHOW DON'T GO TOGETHER.

I THINK THE WHOLE POINT OF THE THING
IS THAT IT IS POINTLESS. THEREFORE I DEEM IT ART.

IT HIDES A MULTITUDE OF SINS

I THINK YOU TOUCHED A NERVE THERE.

I NEVER REALISED WHAT A LONG FACE HE HAD BEFORE NOW
LIKE A HORSE WITHOUT TEETH.

I FOUND MY MUM'S VIBRATOR.
EVEN WORSE, I TRIED IT OUT.

I USE MY FLATMATE'S VEGETABLES TO PLEASURE MYSELF.
THEN I PUT THEM BACK IN THE FRIDGE WITHOUT TELLING HER.

I WOULD INSULT HIM, BUT I THINK NATURE BEAT ME TOO IT

FORMATTING YOUR HARD DISK WILL SOON GET RID OF THIS PROBLEM

PLEASE KEEP THE NOISE DOWN
I DRANK ENOUGH TO SINK A SMALL ISLAND LAST NIGHT.

BUGGER ME BACKWARDS WITH A BROOM HANDLE

IT ALWAYS SEEMS TO BE THE 'L' MISSING.
MAYBE THEY ARE STOLEN FOR HEN PARTIES.

WHY DO FEMALE TEACHERS ALWAYS HAVE MOUSTACHES?

SEVENTY-FIVE PENCE?
TRY TWO-POUND-FIFTY TO THREE-POUNDS THESE DAYS, GRANDDAD

I'VE MET MY SOULMATE AT LAST.
I'M MARRIED TO SOMEONE ELSE, BUT AT LEAST I FOUND HIM.

IT'S THE WORLD'S BEST INVISIBLE WALL NOW
COMPLETELY INVISIBLE FROM SPACE, EARTH, BERLIN, ETC.

MY WIFE SPEAKS FLUENT GERMAN AND ENGLISH
AT PARTIES I GENERALLY SPEAK FLUENT BOLLOCKS, SO I TAKE HER ALONG TO TRANSLATE FOR ME.

THE ONLY TIME WE HAVE GOOD SEX NOW IS AFTER AN ARGUMENT.
WE DON'T ARGUE ENOUGH.

THE BIRDIE SONG ON A ZITHER

BUT I STILL SAY THAT HAND LOOKS VERY TROTTER LIKE.
CHECK FOR A CURLY TAIL

THEY DID IT WITH ANGLED GLASS IN VICTORIAN DAYS

DAMN THAT STUFF IS EVIL
I HAD A WEEKEND OF IT IN LAS VEGAS AND WOKE UP MARRIED.

I FIRST DID IT OUTDOORS IN THE RAIN
NOW WHEN IT RAINS I DON'T TAKE AN UMBRELLA.

IT'S LIKE FRANCE WITHOUT FRENCH PEOPLE.
THAT CAN'T BE A BAD THING.

A MACHINE THAT STUFFS EGGS UP JOHN PRESCOTT'S ARSE AT THE RATE OF THREE A MINUTE?
I'D PAY TO WATCH THAT.

I WOULD LIKE TO BE CALLED 'SIR' JUST ONCE IN MY LIFE
WITHOUT IT BEING FOLLOWED BY THE LINE "I THINK YOU HAD BETTER LEAVE NOW".

THERE ARE TWO GORGEOUS WOMEN IN THE OFFICE, ALWAYS TIGHT TOPS
I CAN'T STOP THINKING OF SMOTHERING MYSELF IN TOMATO KETCHUP AND BEING THEIR SANDWICH FILLING.

I REALLY FANCY A MARRIED MAN,
SADLY, I'M PRETTY SURE HE DOES TOO.

LEAVE IT IN
AND PRETEND IT'S WHAT WE INTENDED

THEY DO WORK BLOODY LONG HOURS AND THEY ARE HARD WORKERS,
AND THEY ARE OPEN TWENTY-FIVE HOURS A DAY.

PULL IT'S TAIL OFF AND SEE IF IT GROWS A NEW ONE
I WANT PROOF IT'S NOT JUST AN URBAN MYTH

STRONG VIAGRA?
HOW DOES THAT WORK?

EITHER GO HUNGRY OR EAT A STUDENT STYLE MEAL.
I SUGGEST A LOT OF ALCOHOL FIRST.

I DIDN'T THINK IT WAS POSSIBLE FOR HIM TO LOOK ANY WEIRDER

SHE THOUGHT I LOOKED LIKE **** ******** (AGEING POP STAR)
I WAS MOST OFFENDED AND SO HAD TO DECLINE THE RATHER TEMPTING OFFER SHE THOUGHT SHE HAD MADE TO HIM

I DON'T HATE YOU
BUT YOU COULD HAVE AT LEAST MATCHED THE DRESS SIZES

LET'S SKIP THE RELATIONSHIP
AND GO STRAIGHT TO THE BREAK-UP SEX.

WOULD YOU LIKE TO SEE ME WEAR MY ANKLES AS EARRINGS?

YOU PUT US TO SHAME AS USUAL

I CAN TELL YOU WHERE HE LIVES IF IT HELPS SPEED UP THE PROCESS
As long as you are not planning on stalking him that is

THAT ANNOYING GUY IN A KILT PLAYING BAGPIPES IN REGENT STREET.
Haven't seen him in ages. Maybe he went to the great bottle in the sky.

BEAUTIFUL IN YOUR SIMPLICITY

IT WAS ME.
But my boyfriend was so drunk he is not sure now whether it was me or anne outside the fire exit. Let him sweat a bit.

MAKE SURE YOU HAVE IT YOUNG
As an adult it's a living nightmare.

BEARD COLOURING GEL?
Do you use it on your beard?

A STUDENT GRANT IS BEER MONEY FOR THE NEXT TERM.

IF YOU DON'T MIND A LITTLE WELL INTENTIONED CRITICISM
It's not the colour that's the problem. Go for something less clingy.

THE NORTH END OF THE COUNTRY IS RATHER TOO SOGGY
And liable to sink if anyone moves there.

FOUR DIFFERENT GUYS HAVE TEXTED ME TODAY ALL WANTING THE SAME THING.
I SHOULD START CHARGING THEM.

MY WIFE SHAVES FOR HER GYNAECOLOGIST,
NEVER FOR ME.

YOU COULD PARK A VW BEETLE IN THERE.
SIDEWAYS.

A TWO YEAR OLD CALLED POPPY ONCE POOPED IN MY POOL.
HAS A NICE RING TO IT, ALL THOSE P's.

I DIDN'T REALISE SHE COULDN'T PLAY GUITAR
AND NOR DID SHE IT SEEMS.

I DON'T UNDERSTAND HOW PEOPLE GET ADDICTED TO PAIN KILLERS.
UNLESS THEY ARE IN PAIN OF COURSE.

OTHER PEOPLE HAVE PUT CORRECTION FLUID ON YOUR SCREEN?
WHO THE FUCK USES CORRECTION FLUID THESE DAYS?

YES, AND LIKE RIDING A BIKE, YOUR FACE CAN GET SMASHED IN.

THERE IS NO RING
YOU CAN BREATHE A SIGH OF RELIEF

HOW'S YOUR HEAD?

We had a guy named 'Shovel' from his head shape,
and another with very large front teeth who we nicknamed 'Tombstones'.

My favourite all time game ruined forever!
I'll never be able to play it again and not think of that.

Cybermen were much scarier than Daleks.

Some of us can barely focus,
let alone recognise satire

She starred in that and got her norks out.
It was all sub-titles. But I don't think anyone noticed.

He was pretending to be someone with no humour
and succeeding.

I had to eat them on survival courses
and I never grew any extra legs or wings.

After a few more scotches
I would probably be able to convince the Beeb that the last twenty
minutes of silence was artistic.

I can't work out which are more painful to look at,
Your legs or those damn ugly shorts.

Did anyone else spend far too long
trying to work out what that spelt as words?

ARE THESE REALLY PROTECT AND SURVIVE IMAGES?
OR A GAY PORN COMIC STRIP?

DON'T BLAME ME IF PEOPLE SIT OUTSIDE YOUR HOUSE
IN A VEHICLE WITH DARKENED WINDOWS FOR A WEEK.

I SEE YOU HAVE SHARED MY PAIN

THE INTERNET IS A PLACE WHERE PEOPLE WITH LIVES
CAN LOSE ARGUMENTS ABOUT LIFE WITH SELF-RIGHTEOUS PEOPLE WHO HAVE NO LIVES.

TRUST ME, WHEN A MAN IS OFFERED A BLOW JOB
HIS CRITERIA DOES NOT INCLUDE WHAT THE WOMAN LOOKS LIKE NAKED.

YOU WANT FRIES WITH THAT TO GO?

I HAVE PEAKED TOO SOON ON OCCASIONS
BUT THAT WAS BLOODY QUICK

HANDBAGS AT DAWN

WAS HIS FATHER DRUNK
WHEN HE WENT TO REGISTER HIS CHILD'S NAME?

I HAVE JUST REALISED THAT TOUCHE
HAS THE WORD 'OUCH' IN THE MIDDLE.

NAKED FAT MEN ARE NOT AMUSING

I REALLY LIKE GIVING BLOW JOBS.
AND I AM TOLD I AM PRETTY GOOD TOO. YOU WANT ME TO PROVE IT?

NOTHING SLIPPED PAST YOU THAT NIGHT
THOUGH IF IT HAD, YOU PROBABLY WOULDN'T BE PREGNANT RIGHT NOW.

NO, STAY AND REVEAL MORE OF YOUR NIGHT TIME EXPLOITS.
YOU STILL HAVE SOME WINE LEFT.

THE ONLY QUESTION THAT SPRINGS TO MIND IS;
MEDICATION TIME?

WE TRIED IT THREE WEEKS AGO
IT LASTED ONE DAY

THIS YEARS EATING CHAMPION WAS A WOMAN
NO SURPRISE THERE.

I DON'T WANT TO SEE YOUR FRIENDS' STUPID FACEBOOK COMMENTS
THAT'S WHY THEY ARE 'YOUR' FRIENDS AND NOT MINE.

IT PUTS EVERYTHING ELSE INTO PERSPECTIVE.

YOU SICK PERSON YOU!

IT FEELS LIKE A MIXTURE OF HAVING YOUR HAIR PULLED OUT
AND WINNING THE LOTTERY

IS SHE A VICTIM OF A FAILED SHRUNKEN HEAD EXPERIMENT?

Her father asked me if my intentions were honourable or not.
I wish I'd known earlier I had a choice.

The farce is strong in this one

How do you determine a dog is depressed?
Dangle a cat in front of it and gauge it's reaction?

I got two in case they were different

It's clinker licking good

Lewd behaviour in a public place?
What exactly is that?

I used to alternate
Gay girl one night
Gay guy the next.
The guys were never a problem, but the girls used to moan so I stopped

Only slightly drunk?
We expect more effort next time. Force yourself.

You should do it for a living.
I mean writing, not being somebody's friend.

Trust me, never swig aftershave. Even if it is 80% alcohol.
It took my throat out and I could not speak for over a day.
My breath smelt good though.

HANDS UP WHERE?

IT COULD DOUBLE AS A SPANKING MACHINE FOR NAUGHTY GIRLFRIENDS

I'M NOT ABOVE WEARING A SHORT SKIRT TO GET THIS THING MOVING.

IT'S AN ILLUSION
CAUSED BY CHEEKS TOO FAR APART.

DID YOU ASSUME THERE WAS A ONE STOP MOUTH SOURCE?

THAT WAS A VERY BRAVE STATEMENT TO MAKE
ONE WE NO DOUBT WILL REMIND YOU OF AGAIN AND AGAIN FOR MONTHS TO COME.

IS IT ME
OR DOES SHE HAVE STRETCH MARKS ON HER LIPS?

HE KEPT HIS HAT ON FOR THE DURATION?

SHE'S NOT SURE WHO THE FATHER IS
SHE SAID SHE WAS LEANING OUT THE CAR WINDOW BEING SICK AT THE TIME OF CONCEPTION.

I PROBABLY WOULDN'T LIKE TO HAVE YOU AS A FRIEND
BUT YOUR MIND FASCINATES ME.

I HOPE YOU CAN ACCOUNT FOR YOUR MOVEMENTS THAT NIGHT

I AM NOT SURE HOW YOU WOULD SAY IT POLITELY.
COMING FROM BEHIND, PERHAPS? STILL SOUNDS RUDE, DOESN'T IT.

SOME OF US ARE STILL TRYING TO FIND IT

I HAVE A THING ABOUT WOMEN'S FINGERS
BUT ONLY IF THEY ARE SMALL. THEY MAKE ME LOOK BIGGER.

YOU HAVE BEEN STARING AT THEM FOR AGES.

I CANNOT COMMENT AS I HAVEN'T SEEN IT.
BUT I AM SURE IT WAS LOVELY.

I GET HOME AND FIND A PORN MAG ON MY PILLOW
I'VE ONLY BEEN GONE A WEEKEND AND ALREADY HE'S FOUND A REPLACEMENT

THE 'BLOW ME' LINE THREW ME

MEN DON'T WANT ROMANCE, THEY WANT SEX.
THE ONLY TIME THEY WRITE POETRY IS WHEN THEY'RE NOT GETTING ANY.

THE ARSEHOLE IS BACK

IF HE EVER COMES TO BED WEARING NOTHING BUT SOCKS AGAIN
HE WON'T NEED TO WORRY ABOUT FATHERING CHILDREN IN FUTURE.

GOODNIGHT?
I HAVE A BOTTLE AND A BALLSACK TO DRAIN FIRST!

SHE IS WELL HUNG FOR A LESBIAN.

EITHER I AM PISSED
OR HE IS WAY OUT OF FOCUS.

SHALL I JOIN THE QUEUE?
I REALLY WOULD LOVE A GO ON THEM.

I LOVE YOU AND WANT TO HAVE ALL YOUR BABIES.
PROVIDING YOU HAVEN'T GOT ANY ALREADY.

WHAT IS THE GUY ON THE RIGHT
ABOUT TO DO TO THAT GIRL BENDING OVER?

IT WAS SO COLD
YOU COULD HAVE HUNG YOUR COAT ON THEM.

I CAN SEE YOUR FATHER'S CONCERNS NOW
PERHAPS IT'S THE KILT

WHAT'S HE GOT AGAINST MEN IN HATS HOLDING SAUSAGES?

THAT WOULD NEED A **LOT** OF BEER!

BEING GAY CURES HEADACHES
STAY AND BE HEALED

THAT LOOKS UNUSUALLY GOOD
FOR THIS HOUR OF THE NIGHT, PROBABLY WON'T SURVIVE DAYLIGHT.

I OFTEN THROW THE WORDS 'SWALLOW', 'PERT', AND 'GUSSET'
INTO CASUAL CONVERSATION FOR THE COMEDY VALUE THEY BRING.

VODKA IS GOOD FOR GETTING UGLY GIRLS INTO BED?
I THOUGHT IT WAS THE OTHER WAY ROUND

HE'S FALLEN ASLEEP
STAPLE HIS TIE TO THE TABLE AND SLAP HIS FACE.

MY FLATMATE ANSWERED A CALL FROM ONE OF THOSE INDIAN CALL CENTRES ASKING IF HE WAS SATISFIED WITH HIS PHONE COMPANY.
HE REPLIED "THANK GOD YOU'VE CALLED. I'M COOKING A CURRY AND I'M HAVING A FEW PROBLEMS".

GOD MADE MEN THINK WITH THEIR DICKS
TO STOP THEM SPENDING EVERY WAKING HOUR DRINKING BEER.

IT WORKED
LOOK AT THE PUBLICITY THEY JUST GOT FROM YOU MENTIONING IT.

I PARTICULARLY LIKED HIS CODPIECE

IT HURT MY MALE PRIDE
FINDING OUT SHE HAD SLEPT WITH MORE WOMEN THAN I HAD.

YOU KNOW THEY ARE NEVER THE SAME PEOPLE,
THEY KEEP CHANGING, SO THE DEAD INDIAN WAS PROBABLY NEVER SEEN AGAIN

CAN BODILY SWEAT EVER BE TRULY AROUSING?

WHERE I COME FROM
POSH CLOTHES ARE ANY THAT HAVEN'T BEEN USED FOR CARRYING COAL

IT HAS TO BE **LIVE** NATURAL YOGHURT, YOU FUCKING IDIOT.
NOT THE STUFF YOU SPREAD ON CEREAL.

I NEVER SAW GOD AS WEARING A PINK BASEBALL CAP IN MY MIND.

I FIND PENGUINS ARE THE WORST
THEY RUIN THE HERBACEOUS BORDERS AND FRIGHTEN NEXT DOORS CAT.

I LIKE TO THINK THE TIGHT SKIRT AND SUSPENDER BELT
COMPENSATE FOR THE TISSUES STUFFED IN MY BRA.

THEY KEPT TRYING TO RUN UNDER MY CAR
NO MATTER WHICH WAY I SWERVED I STILL MISSED THEM.

THEY DON'T MAKE CRAPPY FILMS LIKE THAT ANYMORE, SADLY

I DIDN'T SMILE LIKE THAT
LAST TIME I LOOKED

BRAZILIAN FLAG?
GREEN AND YELLOW WITH A SHORT BROWN STRIP IN THE CENTRE?

SUCH BEAUTY IN SUCH SIMPLICITY.

I HAVEN'T BROACHED THE SUBJECT OF MY WIFE WITH HER YET,
I DON'T THINK IT WOULD GO IN MY FAVOUR SOMEHOW.

I THINK YOU HAVE THE WRONG IDEA ABOUT THIS PLACE.
YOU DO THE WORK, WE INSULT YOU. NOT THE OTHER WAY ROUND.

I DON'T LOOK LIKE THAT.
EXCEPT MAYBE AT SIX O'CLOCK IN THE MORNING

DON'T TELL HER I'M NOT MARRIED
I HAVE MY REASONS.

DO YOU HAVE ANY MONEY?
I'VE PULLED.

WHO IS SHE?
I WOULD, AND SO WOULD MY WIFE

I WOULDN'T HAVE MINDED
IF IT HAD BEEN GOOD OR EVEN FUNNY

GET YOUR WIFE OR GIRLFRIEND TO JOIN IN.
OR BOTH TOGETHER FOR TWICE THE FUN

ISN'T HE AS BAD AS THE PEOPLE HE TRIES TO DISCREDIT?

IT WAS SO POWERFUL
IT BURNT THE WHITE LINES OFF THE ROAD

THEY GET UPSET AT GIRLS KISSING IN HERE.

WHAT A LOVELY THOUGHT JUST BEFORE TEATIME.

I WAS MADE AN HONOURY LESBIAN ONCE
IF I WAS FEMALE I'M SURE I'D BE ONE.

I ALWAYS SEEM TO BUY THREE ROUNDS
BECAUSE SOME PEOPLE ARE TIGHT, SOME ARE POOR, AND SOME DRINK SO FUCKING SLOWLY I WOULD DIE OF THIRST WAITING FOR THEM.

ALL THIS TIME AND COSTLY EDUCATION
AND I NEVER KNEW THAT GOATS LAID EGGS.

THERE IS NOT ENOUGH ALCOHOL IN THE WORLD
TO MAKE ME LET HIM PUT IT THERE.

I VALUE OUR FRIENDSHIP TOO MUCH TO DATE YOU.

HOW STRANGE,
I HAVE ONE OF HIM DOING THAT TOO

BIT OF A BAD HAIR DAY GOING ON HERE.
I GOT OVER EXCITED

SHUT IT, RICKY

YOU REALLY MUST TRY HARDER IN THE MORNINGS.
AND OF COURSE HARDER IN THE MORNINGS IS THE BEST WAY TO BE.

I ASKED MY BOSS "WOULD YOU LIKE TO SAMPLE A MUFFIN, I'VE GOT ENOUGH FOR EVERYONE?"
I'LL NOT BE BRINGING MY HOMEMADE MUFFINS INTO WORK AGAIN.

I DREAD TO THINK WHAT GIRLS YOU GO OUT WITH

I'M SURE THE MILKMAN LEAVES CREAM UP HER BACK ALLEY

IT BETTER BE WORTH IT.
ALL THE EFFORT YOU ARE PUTTING IN.

YOU ARE GOING TO BE IN TROUBLE IF YOU
HAVE TO LOG IN AND TYPE YOUR NAME.

ISN'T IRONY WONDERFUL.

HUMUNGOUS POINTY BREASTS,
UNFEASIBLY NARROW WAISTS, AND STOCKINGS AND SUSPENDERS. I LOVE 50'S STYLES.

IT WAS AFTER A FAILED EXPERIMENT
WITH STRING, EMPTY DISHWASHER LIQUID BOTTLES AND STICKY-BACK PLASTIC.

DOESN'T SEEM TO STOP PEOPLE
LACK OF IDEAS I MEAN.

A KNEE IN THE TESTICLES.
SOLUTION FOR EVERY PROBLEM IN LIFE.

TAKEN FROM US AT A VERY YOUNG AGE
UNDER FORTY I THINK

I'M A BRIT AND AS CONFUSED AS YOU ARE

HE REALLY DID GO BLIND DRINKING A MUG OF COCOA
But only because he forgot to take the spoon out.

WE ARE CURRENTLY BUSY IN THE SOUTH
Watching trees blow down and lakes forming

SOMEWHERE I HAVE THE OUTTAKES
They couldn't include because the people mentioned were still alive.

WE'VE BOTH SACRIFICIED THINGS WE LOVE TO BE IN THIS RELATIONSHIP.
Mine was shopping whenever I liked, his was setting out his Scalextric.

DAMMIT
Now I have the spam song in my head again! Will I never be rid of it.

I WILL NEVER UNDERSTAND
The borderline difference between genius and stupidity.

THE TOWN BIKE?
Ridden by everyone

WHAT HAPPENED TO IT?
Did someone sit on it?

FUCK ME
That man would emotionally disturb me, let alone a child.

IT WAS MEANT TO BE HUMOROUS
Or failing that, understanding.

THE HOST SERVICES THEM ALL AND THEN SPITS THEM OUT...
I'M DESPERATELY HOPING IT'S A WILD PARTY AND NOT SOME GEEKY IT THING.

ONE WEEK IS DISRESPECTFUL FOR ANY WOMAN TO DEPRIVE A MAN
IF THIS PERIOD HAS EXPIRED WITHOUT GOOD EXCUSE, SUCH AS CHILDBIRTH, THEN A MAN IS FULLY ENTITLED TO EXPLORE PASTURES NEW.

YOU HAVE ME SCRATCHING NOW

I HAVE NOT TURNED MINE OFF NOW FOR OVER FOUR WEEKS
AND IT HAS NEVER MELTED.

DRINK DOES THAT TO YOU

THE SONG THAT PROMOTES DRINK DRIVING
AND THEN RUNS OUT OF LYRICS.

I'M THINKING OF A YOUNGER MODEL WITH A BIT MORE GO IN IT.
ONE THAT TRIES THAT BIT HARDER ON A MORE REGULAR BASIS.

IT'S GOTTA BE WORTH A SHOT DEVELOPING THEM,
ANY TOPLESS?

HE IS HALF ALIEN, HALF FOREIGN AND HALF NOT THERE.

I HAVE THE SAME PROBLEM WHEN I WAKE UP
IT LOOKS BIGGER THAN WHEN I WENT TO BED.

WHAT COLOUR WERE YOUR LEGS BEFORE THE TROUSERS RAN?

BLOODY NHS
SAVING ALL THE GOOD DRUGS FOR THE NURSES PARTY NEXT WEEKEND.

YOU WANT TO HEAR I'D HAVE PREFERRED TO STAY BROKE AND SINGLE.
SORRY GIRLS, A RICH HUSBAND I'VE ONLY GOT TO PUT UP WITH WEEKENDS WINS
HANDS DOWN ANY DAY.

IT WENT OFF IN MY HAND
IT'S BEEN DOING THAT A LOT RECENTLY.

IT'S ALL DOWNHILL FROM HERE

AN OSTRICH EGG IS IMPOSSIBLE TO EAT IN ONE GO.
EVEN WITH MY MOUTH.

I SAW A WOMAN WEARING A T-SHIRT THAT SAID
"FUCK FOOTBALL
FUCK ME INSTEAD"
BUT SHE WOULDN'T LET ME

RABBIT IS CLOSER TO CHICKEN THAN DOG
IN FLAVOUR YOU IDIOT!

YOUR MIND SCARES ME AND EXCITES ME IN ONE STRANGE EMOTION.

THEY'RE LOVELY TO LOOK AT
AND I HAVE BEEN LOOKING AT THEM FAR TOO LONG NOW

AND THERE I STOOD WITH A HALF-TRIMMED HEDGE
AND NO, THAT ISN'T A EUPHEMISM.

I WILL REMEMBER YOUR DEFINITION OF CLEAVAGE
FOR FUTURE DEFENCE AGAINST THE WIFE. THANK YOU.

WHAT THE LORD HAS FORGOTTEN,
WE MAKE UP IN COTTON WOOL AND TISSUE PAPER.

I WALKED THE TWO MILES TO THE BANK LUNCHTIME
IT WAS INSPIRING. SO MUCH SO I STOPPED IN EVERY PUB ON THE WAY BACK - SIX IN TOTAL - AND HAD A PINT. I AM NOW HAPPY, SUNBURNT AND PISSED. AND I'VE SPENT EVERY PENNY I GOT OUT.

I'M SORRY I NEVER MET YOU BEFORE I GOT MARRIED.
I WOULD HAVE ROGERED YOU SENSELESS.

ONLY NANNY WHIPLASH IS ALLOWED THE CHEESE GRATER.

I PISSED ON THE BOSSES RADIATOR.
SOMETHING TO REMEMBER ME BY ON THOSE COLD DAYS.

MUST BE ONE HELL OF A WOMAN
THAT CAN TAKE A SIX FOOT VIBRATOR. PERHAPS IT'S A PRINTING ERROR.

HE LOOKED JUST THE SAME FORTY YEARS AGO?
IS THAT MAN NINETY YEARS OLD NOW?

I'M NOT HAVING PROBLEMS
- WELL NOTHING MODERN MEDICAL PRACTICES CAN'T COPE WITH

I ONLY LET YOU BECAUSE
YOU WERE THE FIRST GUY WHO MADE ME FEEL PRETTY WHEN I WAS SOBER.

I GOT HALF A BLOW JOB LAST NIGHT
DOES THAT COUNT AS SEX?

IT LOOKS FEMALE
BUT ONLY JUST

TOMATOES ALWAYS KNOW WHEN I'M WEARING NEW CLOTHES.

I LOVE THESE MIXED CAMPS OF LOVE AND HATE.

THAT'S WORTH TEN FREE BEERS IN A HOSTELRY OF YOUR CHOICE.
JUST WINK AND TELL THEM DORIS THE HORSE SENT YOU, THEY'LL UNDERSTAND.

I'D GIVE ANYTHING TO SLEEP WITH A BEAUTIFUL WOMAN FOR ONCE
INSTEAD OF MY WIFE OR A CHEAP HOOKER.

IT'S AN ARTICLE BY THE INSTITUTE OF MADE-UP STATISTICS

YOURS IS EVEN WORSE THAN MINE.
BUT IT MADE ME SMILE.

WERE YOU SURPRISED UNEXPECTEDLY BY A HORSE AS A CHILD?

IS THAT PUPPIES AS IN 'PERT'
OR AS IN 'SLOBBERING BUT CUTE'?

OH, BUGGER!
I'LL HAVE TO DESTROY MY 'DOWN WITH PACIFICA' BANNERS. I AM SO YESTERDAY.

I GET BONUS POINTS FOR LOSING IT IN A MINI
I MANAGED IT BECAUSE SHE WAS SO AGILE AND BENDY. I HAD VERY LITTLE TO DO WITH THE MATTER REALLY.

I KNEW A GIRL WHOSE HAIR WAS SO BLACK IT WAS BLUE.

YOU CAN GAUGE MY ABILITY BY THE LIPSTICK-RING DEPTH MARKS

I'M RUNNING SHORT OF NURSES
STARCHED WHITE OUTFIT, STOCKINGS, SUSPENDERS, SOFT HANDS, YOU KNOW THE KIND

BEST SOURCE OF FREE PORN ON THE NET
SO I AM TOLD

WHEN I FIRST SET EYES ON HIM I KNEW HE WAS THE ONLY MAN FOR ME.
WHEN HE LEFT THIS MORNING HE TOLD ME HE WAS MARRIED

I'D FEEL SAFER WITH MR BEAN IN CHARGE OF THE ECONOMY.

MY NAME'S ONLY FOUR LETTERS LONG
AND THE PRESS STILL MANAGED TO GET IT WRONG.

I GUESSED FROM THE STANDARD OF YOUR PREVIOUS WORK
THIS WAS AN ACCIDENT.

I AM ALWAYS AMAZED AT HOW MINOR MIDDLE MANAGERS
ACT AS IF IT IS THEIR COMPANY, WHEN THEY ARE BUT MERE MINIONS WITH A SLIGHTLY BIGGER HAT

PERHAPS IT'S AN INVISIBLE FRIEND
THAT NO ONE ELSE CAN SEE.

THE PROBLEM WITH MORNING SPOONING IS MORNING BREATH.

MY PROBLEM IS NOT SO MUCH HIM FORGETTING THINGS
IT'S HIM REMEMBERING THINGS THAT NEVER HAPPENED, AT LEAST — NOT WITH ME.

MY SITE WAS CLOSED DOWN
AFTER RECEIVING 30,000 INSULTS IN ONE HOUR.

I'LL WET THE BABIES HEAD FOR YOU
I EXPECT YOU TO RETURN THE COMPLIMENT

THEY ADOPT DESIGNER LABELS THAT ARE OBVIOUS FROM THE OUTSIDE
THAT WAY THEY CAN BE SPOTTED A MILE AWAY.

TWO OF YOU WOULD BE TOO MUCH TO TAKE IN ONE LIFETIME.
I STILL WOULD THOUGH. TOGETHER. LIFE TIME AMBITION STILL TO ACHIEVE.

NO, NO, NO, NO, NO!
A SIZE 40 WOMAN SHOULD NEVER POSE FOR EROTIC UNDERWEAR!

HE'S ONLY GOT TO LOOK AT THE CAMERA WITH HIS SCARY EYES.
I SHIT MY PANTS.

THE SCORE BOARDS THEY HOLD UP
ARE FOR STYLE, TECHNICAL ABILITY, AND BOUNCE FACTOR

FOR YOUR BIRTHDAY SHE IS GIVING YOU A 'RODEO NIGHT'?
IS THAT WHERE SHE TOSSES YOU OFF IN UNDER FIVE SECONDS?

ROASTING IN THE LOUNGE?
I SEE WHAT YOU MEAN, FOOTBALLERS WOULD NOT BE SEEN DEAD IN THE KITCHEN.

MONEY DOESN'T BUY LOVE, HEALTH OR HAPPINESS.
BUT IT DOES BRING GREAT PARTIES, GREAT LOOKING WOMEN, AND GREAT HOLIDAYS

PROFESSOR PLUM UP THE BUM IN THE BALLROOM?

IT WENT 'WHOOSH'.
STRAIGHT OVER HER HEAD.

ROMEO, ROMEO
WHERE THE FUCK ARE YOU, ROMEO?

I WAS IN THE MIDDLE OF A SURPRISE ATTACK FROM THE REAR
WHEN SHE SPOTTED THE MISSING REMOTE UNDER THE SOFA. I'LL BE OUT OF ACTION FOR AT LEAST A WEEK.

IF YOU DO HAVE TO DO THAT
I'D RATHER YOU KEPT THE DETAILS TO YOURSELF.

YOU SPOTTED THE DELIBERATE ERROR
IN MY SUGGESTION HE HAS A MATE.

I DID HEAR THAT HE WAS KNOWN FOR HIS FONDNESS OF LITTLE BOYS
AND TOO MUCH MAKE-UP

I MET A BOY FROM BIRKENHEAD WHO IS POSSIBLY TATTOOED.
I HATE WHEN SMITHS LYRICS COME TRUE.

THEY MEASURED HER FACE AND FOUND IT TO BE MATHEMATICALLY THE CLOSEST TO PERFECTION.
LIKE US MEN ARE LOOKING AT HER FACE???

YOU CAN TELL WIMBLEDON HAS STARTED
IT'S FUCKING POURING.

I HAD A REALLY STRANGE DREAM THE OTHER NIGHT
ABOUT GETTING COME ON MY FACE. IT MADE NO SENSE BECAUSE NOTHING WAS TOUCHING HIM. I WAS LYING ON MY BACK AND HE WAS ABOVE ME AND MOVING LIKE HE WAS HAVING SEX BUT WITHOUT ANYTHING TOUCHING HIM.
THEN HE CAME AND IT LANDED ON MY FACE. IT WAS MOST UNEXPECTED...
WHY HAS IT GONE SO QUIET IN HERE?

IT WAS THE REMAINS OF UNCLE VESPAR
I WONDERED WHERE THAT TIN HAD GONE.

NOT TILL YOU'VE SWORN ALLEGIANCE IN BLOOD
AND BARED AT LEAST ONE BUTTOCK TO THE QUEEN.

THAT GAME - AND THE SCORE -
TOOK ME SO BY SURPRISE I HAD TO BE CARRIED HOME.

I WOULD, BUT THE FOOTBALL IS STARTING.
THERE MAY BE A SHORTAGE OF ENGLISH SPOKEN HERE FOR A WHILE.

SOMEONE THREW A HALF EATEN MEAT PIE AT THE LINESMAN
HALF EATEN MAKES IT TWICE AS FUNNY.

YOU KNOW THE PROCEDURE BY NOW.
BEND DOWN. GRAB YOUR ANKLES

WHAT DO YOU MEAN, YOU CAN READ MY LIPS THROUGH MY TROUSERS?

IT'S A MEKON FROM DAN DARE COMICS FROM THE '50S.
AND NO I AM NOT OLD ENOUGH TO HAVE READ THEM WHEN THEY FIRST CAME OUT.

ONCE YOU SLEEP WITH SOMEONE,
YOU CAN NEVER BE NORMAL FRIENDS AGAIN. EVER.

THE TROUBLE WITH A HARPSICHORD IS THERE IS NO VOLUME CONTROL

I HAVE BEEN WAITING TWENTY MINUTES
FOR THE BALL TO KNOCK THE STICKY THING OFF THE OTHER STICKS.

FOR AGES I THOUGHT "COME ON TIM" WAS A BUKKAKE VIDEO.

DEDICATION IN YOUR TIRELESS QUEST.
FUTILE, BUT I ADMIRE IT.

HAIRY BACKS ARE ONLY SEXY IF YOU ARE A GORILLA

LIFE JUST WENT OUT OF SYNC FOR ME AGAIN
LIKE THE WINDSCREEN WIPERS ON THE CAR TO CERTAIN MUSIC TRACKS, THEY SEEM TO BE IN PERFECT TIME THEN DRIFT OUT.

THE POOR GUY GETS SHOT EVERY TIME I WATCH THAT FILM.
YOU'D THINK HE WOULD LEARN.

I KNOW
She told me how small you are

I USED TO HAVE FANTASIES ABOUT THAT WOMAN
If she knew the things she has done with me she would have me arrested.

POOR GEORGE
Fed up being squeezed into cocktail dresses

I MISS THE SMELL AND TASTE OF YOU.

NOT SURE WHICH WORRIES ME MORE...
The fact that these exist, or you finding them.

NEXT TIME PUT IT IN THE SHALLOW END.
That sounds quite rude doesn't it?

THIS WON'T TAKE LONG
Just think of England.

I KNOW WHEN I GET REALLY LUCKY,
My shirt and pants get ironed next morning.

GO TO THE LADIES AND PUT YOUR KNICKERS IN YOUR HANDBAG,
You won't be needing them tonight.

I TOLD HER SHE SHOULD TRY PHONE SEX.
Long story short. Vibrate function. Washed her phone after, now it stopped working and she blames me for her being so thick!

I wasn't fondling you.
It's called finding your way in the dark

Deep breath,
think fluffy thoughts

You had to say it out loud, didn't you?

Let's have a girl's night out.
We'll get smashed, buy a shitload of stuff from Ann Summers and spend the night learning how to use it.

It fucks up your mind
if you are in any way susceptible to fucking up.

Does your mother know she is world famous now?
On the internet anyway

The girls loved being in a real darkened studio
and after much vodka would often end up thanking us males in a way only females can.

That would be the sound of the Swedish plumber
coming to fix the plotline of a 70s titty movie

Half a lager and a bag of pork scratchings
Works a treat in Keighley

I always use a keyboard condom.
One can never be too sure.

ONE LEGGED WOMAN.
NEW POSSIBILITIES IN POSITIONING

IS IT TRUE WHAT THEY SAY ABOUT BIG FEET?

BIG SIGN ON THE COAL SAID 'NEVER USE YOUR BARBECUE INDOORS'
I COULDN'T HELP WONDER WHAT TYPE OF PERSON SUDDENLY GETS THE DESIRE TO
WHEEL THE BBQ INTO THE LIVING ROOM AND LIGHT IT.

DOES 'YOU KNOW WHAT' INVOLVE BUGGERY?

IN SPACE, NO ONE CAN HEAR YOU FART

HOW TIGHT ARE DUCKS ARSES? GENERALLY?
JUST IN THE NAME OF RESEARCH, OF COURSE.

YOUR SURFING HISTORY IS STORED IN AN AREA OF HARD DISK
SET ASIDE FOR SUCH PURPOSES, SO THAT OTHER PEOPLE CAN CHECK IF YOU HAVE
BEEN LOOKING AT BREASTS.

I DREW A MAN WITH A WILLY ON HIS HEAD AND HIS EYES WERE BOOBS
I REALLY NEED TO GROW UP SOMETIMES, I'M 37 FOR GOD'S SAKE.

WHAT A WONDERFUL PUBLIC SERVICE MESSAGE THAT WAS FOR .US ALL

I HAVE THE PERFECT SHAPED FACE FOR A HOOD

I SHOULDN'T HAVE LIKED THAT AS MUCH AS I DID
THE THOUGHT POLICE WILL BE AFTER ME NOW.

GO ON, HAVE A HISSY FIT
THROW ALL YOUR TOYS OUT THE PRAM

ARE YOU SURE YOU HAVE ANY FRIENDS?

I GOT SO DRUNK IN BELGUIM THAT I LOST A WEEK OF MY LIFE
AND A TWO WEEK OLD CAR WHICH I DRUNKENLY LENT TO A BELGIAN I HAD ONLY MET THAT EVENING TO COLLECT HIS GIRLFRIEND. HE BROKE THE CLUTCH - RIGHT HAND DRIVE - AND THEN COULDN'T REMEMBER WHERE HE LEFT IT. NOT A GREAT WEEK.

IS THE MATRIX NOT REAL?
NO WONDER MY LEGS HURT WHEN I JUMP OFF TALL BUILDINGS...

I NEED TO CUT BACK ON CHEESE AT BEDTIME

DID YOU COP A CHEEKY FEEL?

A TYRE IRON UP THE JACKSY IS QUITE GOOD REVENGE.
NOT VERY SUBTLE THOUGH.

DID HIS LEGS SHRINK IN THE WASH?

THAT GETS MORE DISTURBING EVERY TIME I WATCH IT

I HOPE IT LASTS LONGER THAN MINE.
MINE GOT A PUNCTURE

DOUBLE ENTRY?
ARE YOU SURE SHE'S JUST AN ACCOUNTANT?

I REALLY DON'T GET THIS
IS THERE SOMETHING I AM MISSING?

AFTER LARGE QUANTITIES OF SUSPICIOUS SUBSTANCES
...YES.

IT'S A FRENCH CHIPPY THEN
IF IT SELLS FRENCH FRIES

I CAME HERE TO FORGET THE FOOTBALL

HAS HE EMBARRASSED HIMSELF AGAIN?
ANYONE GOT ANY TISSUES?.

HE HAS THAT GLOW
OF ONE WHO LIVES NEAR A NUCLEAR POWER STATION

RING BINDERS
THAT GET TO 80% FULL AND THEN RANDOMLY VOMIT THEIR CONTENTS ON THE FLOOR, JUST WHEN YOU'RE ON THE WAY TO A MEETING.

I HATE STAPLERS THAT REFUSE TO STAPLE ALL THE WAY THROUGH
MANGLING THE CORNER OF THE DOCUMENT YOU'VE JUST PRINTED ON THE 'SPECIAL PAPER'.

HAVE THEY BEEN SAT ON?
EVERY PAIR I HAVE EVER OWNED HAVE BEEN SAT ON

IMAGINE IT PLAYED TOPLESS

IF I SEE A PROGRAM ABOUT A DEADLY ILLNESS,
I ALWAYS HAVE ALL THE SYMPTOMS AND WORRY. IMAGINE BEING A DOCTOR AND
KNOWING ALL THE SYMPTOMS TO EVERY ILLNESS?

NAKED BOWLS
BY OLD AGE PENSIONERS BEATS IT BY MILES. HORRIBLE.

SHE DOES HAVE LARGE LIPS.

YOU NOW *REALISE* YOU ARE GETTING PISSED AFTER THREE PINTS.
YOU GOT THE SAME EFFECT WHEN YOU WERE A STUDENT, BUT THEN THIS WAS A
BONUS NOT A THINKING POINT.

I DREAD TO THINK WHAT NUN BUTTER IS.

DO THINGS OFTEN COME INTO YOUR HEAD?

THE SOUND A BUILDER MAKES
WHEN A LARGE BREASTED WOMAN WALKS PAST.

I MADE THE SAME STUPID MISTAKE YESTERDAY
I'LL PROBABLY MAKE IT AGAIN TOMORROW..

MY JOB IS DONE, I CAN RELAX.
THE CLINK OF ICE, THE FRESHLY POURED SINGLE MALT, THE SMILE, THE BELCH.

SPRING AND CHICKEN
ARE NOT THE WORDS I WOULD HAVE CHOSEN.

I PISS IN THE POOL ALL THE TIME, IT'S NEVER GONE PURPLE,
AND IT'S A LOVELY WARM FEELING DOWN MY LEGS.

SINCE YOU'RE NOT HAVING ONE I'LL HAVE ONE FOR YOU,
CHEERS.

YES, BUT TO SAVE TIME REVERSE THE FILM
AND WATCH THE GOOD BITS FIRST

IF I HAVE ONE MORE DRINK AND SAY SOMETHING STUPID
WILL YOU HOLD IT AGAINST ME?

I WOULDN'T
ALTHOUGH SHE DOES HAVE AN INTERESTINGLY LARGE MOUTH.

THERE ARE NO BLUE SMARTIES!

I CANNOT GET THOSE FISH
FROM *THE MEANING OF LIFE* OUT MY HEAD NOW

THIS IS PROBABLY NOT THE RIGHT PLACE FOR A SENSIBLE ANSWER
OR PERHAPS THAT IS WHAT YOU WANTED.

HOW MUCH DO THEY GET PAID A WEEK
TO PASS THE BALL STRAIGHT TO THE OPPOSITION?

I WILL PROBABLY GO FIND IT NOW,
AND MAKE A CHOICE I'LL REGRET.

THAT WAS ONE HELL OF A CONFESSION TO MAKE

SHE DID HAVE KNOCKERS BIGGER THAN HER HEAD,
SO IT WAS AN INEVITABLE CAREER MOVE.

I LOST MY VOTING CARD TO AN ENTHUSIASTIC TWO YEAR OLD

WONDERFUL WARPED HUMOUR
MORE LIKE THIS FROM EVERYONE PLEASE.

THANK GOODNESS MY WIFE DOESN'T SEE WHAT I POST ONLINE

THE HAND MOVEMENT INSIDE THE TROUSERS IS EXCELLENT.

IT'S SO DIFFICULT BEING BI
LESBIANS DON'T TAKE ME SERIOUSLY AND MEN JUST WANT THREESOMES.

YOU ARE SO TURNING INTO EVERYTHING YOU HATE ABOUT LONDON.

I BROKE UP HIS MARRIAGE AND NOW I DON'T WANT HIM.
I GUESS I JUST LIKE THE THRILL OF THE CHASE.

IT'S ROAD TRAFFIC ACCIDENT TV
I HATE TO ADMIT IT IS WATCHABLE. BUT DON'T TELL ANYONE I SAID SO.

WERE YOU THE GUY PEEKING OVER THE URINALS?

ARE THEY UP HIS SHIRT OR DID HE EAT ALL THE PIES?

ANYONE CARE FOR A STIFF ONE?

SORRY TO PISS ON YOUR BONFIRE

I SPY WITH MY LITTLE EYE
SOMETHING MISSING

HE ONLY WANTS GIRLS IN WARM CARDIGANS AND SENSIBLE SHOES.

I DON'T GET OUT OF BED FOR LESS THAN TEN PINTS

CAN YOU STAND ON YOUR FRONT KNEE?

I KNOW THAT FEELING.
YOU FEEL GREAT THEN TRY TO WALK TO THE TOILETS BANGING OFF THE WALLS.

THERE IS A REAL DANGER OF SCOUTMASTERS
BEING PUSHED UNDER TRAINS NOW THE SUMMER HOLIDAYS ARE UPON US.

I SAW IT EARLIER
YOU NAUGHTY PERSON YOU

"BEING A MAN SOLICITING A WOMAN
FOR THE PURPOSES OF PROSTITUTION FROM A MOTOR VEHICLE WHILE IT WAS IN A STREET OR PUBLIC PLACE". HE WAS ON A SCOOTER. MAKING THAT STATEMENT SEEM EVEN MORE RIDICULOUS

A PERSON ON ALL FOURS, NAKED.
YOU REST THE DRINKS ON THEIR BACK.

I'VE DECIDED TO START MY MIDLIFE CRISIS EARLY
AND GET IT OVER AND DONE WITH

COULD YOU STUDY HER ANATOMY ANY CLOSER?

I THOUGHT I WOULD TRY MY HAND AT SWIMWEAR DESIGN

TAKE PLEASURE IN THE LITTLE THINGS.

A LONG AS IT IS CLEAN AND FREE OF TEETH
IT CAN BE SHAVEN OR UNSHAVEN FOR ALL I CARE.

I DIDN'T NOTICE THE TRACK SUIT.
I AM WAITING FOR HER BAPS TO FALL OUT.

MY LADY HAS THE PEACHIEST ARSE AND LONGEST LEGS
THAT EVER HAD THE PLEASURE OF SITTING ON MY FACE.

YOU KNOW
I NEVER NOTICED UNTIL YOU BENT OVER.

NEVER LEAVE YOUR PHONE ON THE TABLE
THEN WE MIGHT 'ACCIDENTALLY' GET TO SEE THE PICS OF YOUR WIFE NAKED.

I KEEP VISUALISING THAT IN A WING MIRROR.
QUITE SHOCKING TO SEE WHILE DRIVING.

I COULDN'T KEEP IT IN MY HEAD ANY LONGER...
OR MY TROUSERS

SHE COULD TUCK HER TITS IN HER PANTS.

I FORGOT TO TURN MY SPEAKERS DOWN FROM EARLIER IN THE DAY
SMASHED MY KNEE UNDER THE DESK, SPILT MY DRINK AND POKED MY PEN UP MY NOSE. TOOK SOME EXPLAINING.

YOU KNOW WHAT THEY SAY,
BEHIND EVERY GREAT MAN STANDS A WOMAN GREAT IN BED.

PINK OBOE?

I AM NOT SAYING SHE IS STRETCHED,
BUT IT IS COSTING ME A FORTUNE IN WRISTWATCHES AND NOW EVERY HOUR SHE IS LIKE A PERFORMANCE ARTIST'S RENDITION OF DARK SIDE OF THE MOON.

NOTHING PERSONAL.
WORDS THAT ALWAYS FOLLOW A PARTICULARLY PERSONAL STATEMENT

THEY'RE ALL DOWN OXFORD STREET POINTING DOWN SIDE TURNINGS,
BUT I'M SURE THERE ARE NO GOLF SHOPS DOWN THERE.

I'VE GOT TWO HOSTS GONE DOWN TONIGHT.
THAT SOUNDED INCREDIBLY RUDE FOR SUCH A GEEKY STATEMENT.

DP = DIRECTOR OF PHOTOGRAPHY NOT DOUBLE PENETRATION
WHAT KIND OF FILM DO YOU THINK WE ARE MAKING HERE?

HER SPIRIT FOR ADVENTURE,
LACK OF FEAR AND WILLINGNESS TO RISE TO A CHALLENGE MAKES ME WANT HER

I CAN'T HELP WONDERING
HOW MANY BREASTS A 'LIFE LONG SUPPLY' CONSTITUTES?

I'LL HAVE WHAT SHE'S HAVING.
IT DOESN'T SEEM TO MAKE HER FAT.

NORMALLY I AM STILL AWAKE FROM THE NIGHT BEFORE
BUT TODAY I AM UP EARLY. OO-ER MISSUS!

I KEEP MY HELMET POLISHED AND READY AT ALL TIMES
BE PREPARED IS MY MOTTO..

THE PROVERBIAL PERFECT FACE FOR RADIO

YOU COULD START OFF BY EXPLAINING
THAT SHE IS HIS LONG LOST SISTER ON HIS STEPFATHER'S, EX-WIFE'S, SISTER'S SIDE

LEAVE THEM ON
THAT WAY NO ONE WILL STEAL YOUR SOCKS.

MAKE MINE STRONG, DARK AND SWEET
LIKE A DUSKY MAIDEN

IF ONLY I KNEW WHO SHE WASN'T

WHY DO I ALWAYS FALL FOR MEN WHO ARE EITHER
GAY, MARRIED OR TWICE MY AGE?

THAT'S NOT WHAT YOUR BOYFRIEND TOLD US.

SOGGY BISCUIT
Don't ask! And never Google it.

It must be tough getting girls with a light bulb head.

If you leave me for him,
I lose nothing and you gain nothing.

I see people who look like that
after 3am at certain parties. It may just be me.

The dregs of society gathered together in one room.
Can of petrol and a match anyone?

I met her once
she is about seventeen feet tall

The question is
which thirty percent of him is gay?

My wife is gay
I bring girls home and she sleeps with them too.

Did you ever appear in that black and white film
Children of the Damned?

When we're in the shower together,
I piss down the back of his legs without telling him. My revenge for putting up with his stuff running down my legs.

I'M NOT ALLOWED POINTY THINGS

I HAVE NO IDEA WHO HE IS OR HOW HE KNOWS I LIKE IT THAT WAY.

JUST PUT HIM DOWN SLOWLY
AND KEEP YOUR HANDS WHERE WE CAN SEE THEM.

I FOUND A COLOURING BOOK TODAY
HAD TO TRY IT OUT.

HER SOFT FURNISHINGS ARE LOOKING A BIT SCRUFFY
TIME FOR SOME VAGINAL REJUVENATION TO BE RID OF THAT BURST SOFA.

I COULDN'T STOP STARING AT IT, IT WAS EATING MY CRISPS.

I DON'T CARE WHAT YOUR NAME IS,
GET THOSE FUCKING REINDEER OFF MY ROOF

I AM EATING THEM NOT OUT OF NECESSITY
BUT BECAUSE SOMEONE PUT THEM IN FRONT OF ME

ALL THE STARS I EVER SLEPT WITH WERE CRAP IN BED.
THE TELLTALE STORIES IN THE PAPERS ARE A PACK OF LIES.

IN MY HEAD IT WAS MORE ALONG THE LINES
"SHOW ME YOURS AND I'LL SHOW YOU MINE"

I HAVE NO IDEA WHO YOU ARE
SO YOU CAN SAY WHAT YOU REALLY FEEL

PISS ON IT,
MY DOGS ANSWER TO LIFE.

WERE THESE FOUR 'LOVELY' GUYS
CALLED, RICK, VIVIAN, MIKE AND NEIL BY ANY CHANCE?

I HAVE A SUSPICIOUS STAIN ON MY JEANS I HAVE ONLY JUST NOTICED
THIS MAY IN PART EXPLAIN WHY I WAS SHUNNED IN WAITROSE EARLIER

YOU'VE HEARD OF BOSOM BUDDIES?
WELL COLIN IS BILL'S BUTTOCK BUDDY.

NOW I AM STUCK WITH THAT IMAGE
OF A BIG DANGLING BALL-SACK FOR THE REST OF THE EVENING.

YOU SEEM TO BE INTENT ON MAKING ME BLUSH THIS EVENING.
I MUST ADMIT THAT YOU'VE NOT BEEN ENTIRELY UNSUCCESSFUL.

THIS GIVES ME SATISFACTION, I CANNOT DENY IT.
AND I DO LIKE SATISFACTION. GIVING AS WELL AS RECEIVING.

PEOPLE THINK I'M QUIET AND SHY.
THEY SHOULD SEE ME LAP DANCING AFTER THREE LARGE VODKA AND RED BULLS

CASHIER NUMBER THREE PLEASE.

YOU'RE RIGHT,
IT'S NOT OFTEN YOU FIND A WINDOW TO ANOTHER WORLD IN YOUR GARDEN

IT LOOKS THE KIND OF THING YOU WOULD DO AND THEN DENY.

DON'T YOU JUST LOVE CONVERSATIONS
THAT MAKE SO LITTLE SENSE YOU THINK YOU UNDERSTAND THEM.

THAT'S SOMETHING I CAN RELATE TO,
EVEN THOUGH I'VE NEVER LICKED A LAMPPOST.

I AM SURE THERE IS A HIDDEN MEANING IN EVERYTHING

I'M NOT A VIRGIN
BUT I'VE NEVER KISSED A GIRL PROPERLY.

HARRY HAS GOT THE SACK FOR LOOKING TOO OLD.

I ATE SOAP AND COULDN'T SIT DOWN FOR A WEEK.

LOVELY WAS NOT A WORD THAT SPRANG TO MIND

SADLY MY MUM DID IT MORE THAN ONCE.

DON'T YOU HATE THESE EMBARRASSING MOMENTS OF NON SILENCE

SOMEONE, SOMEWHERE IN HIS FAMILY HISTORY SLEPT WITH A RELATIVE.

I WANT TO GO OUT WITH HIM
JUST TO HAVE THE PLEASURE OF DUMPING HIM AFTER.

I FEEL SO SOILED FOR BEING EARLY

NO GENITALIA LOOKS GOOD WHEN DOING THE SPLITS

THEY GOT FOUND OUT,
THEY HAD BOYFRIENDS

IF I AM HONEST
YOU ARE NOT INSTANTLY MEMORABLE

THE PART CALLS FOR A NEANDERTHAL
YOU SEEM OVER QUALIFIED.

I DIDN'T SEE THE POINT, BUT OTHERS DON'T AGREE WITH ME,
WHICH IS WHAT MAKES THE WORLD GO ROUND.

BLOODY HELL
THAT'S GOOD

DO YOU HAVE A TATTOO ON YOUR ARSE?
YOU REMIND ME OF SOMEONE I HAD FORGOTTEN ABOUT.

YOU CAN'T GET INTO FILMS UNLESS YOU WENT TO THE RIGHT SCHOOL,
JUST LIKE YOU CAN'T SUPPORT MILLWALL UNLESS YOU NEVER WENT TO SCHOOL.

WELL NOW IT IS GONE THEY WILL LOVE IT EVEN MORE.

GO FOR BLUE RINSE, BABY

MINE AREN'T CREATIVE OR ACCURATE
BUT I STILL MAKE PEOPLE SUFFER WITH THEM.

I HURT MY PARTNER TWO DAYS AGO,
BEST TWO DAYS PEACE AND QUIET I'VE HAD IN AGES

I DON'T THINK YOU REALIZE HOW LITTLE YOU GIVE ME TO WORK WITH.

A ONE PERSON FAN CLUB IS A STALKER
IF WE ARE BRUTALLY HONEST ABOUT IT

I STILL THINK 'KIDDIE FIDDLERS' IS A GOOD NAME FOR A BAND.

SHE AIN'T GOT NOBODY,
AND SHE LOOKS SURPRISINGLY HAPPY.

I AM SO SORRY FOR LAUGHING
TOO LOUDLY AND LONG AT THAT STATEMENT

LOOKS LIKE AN EX-GIRLFRIEND
WHO TURNED OUT TO BE WEIRD AND STALKED ME

GREAT EXCUSE TO HAVE TWO NAKED WOMEN
INSTEAD OF ONE

WHAT IS THAT SUSPICIOUS LOOKING PINK OBJECT?

YOU EVIL, EVIL BOY YOU

I NEED AN L-PLATE

FUCK ME THAT'S HAIRY.

ARE WE ALLOWED 'NAKED HOUR'?

HAVE ANOTHER ONE TO DREAM ABOUT

THE HOSPITAL FOUND NOTHING WRONG WITH HER
EXCEPT FOR A CAST IRON ALIBI.

CURSES!
WE'VE BEEN FOILED.

HOW DO YOU THINK THESE THINGS UP?

ITS ARSE WAS ALL OVER THE PLACE.
LIKE A DUCK ON A PLATE OF SNOT.

I KNOW A WOMAN
WHO LOOKS JUST LIKE HIM.

CONSENSUS IS WE DON'T KNOW HOW TO CELEBRATE ST GEORGE'S DAY.
I'M GONNA HUNT DOWN A DRAGON. I USED TO DATE ONE. WHERE'S MY ADDRESS BOOK...

IT'S QUITE INCREDIBLE
THE AMOUNT OF IN-DEPTH KNOWLEDGE OF SHEEP SHAGGING HERE

THAT WILL BE INTERESTING
SEEING AS TWO OF THEM ARE DEAD.

I ALWAYS AGREE TO TAKE PHOTOS OF TOURISTS AND STRANGERS
BUT I ALWAYS MAKE SURE I CUT OFF THEIR HEADS

I CAN'T DECIDE WHICH IS FUNNIEST
PEOPLE USING THE WORD 'PRETENTIOUS' TO MEAN SOMETHING THEY DON'T UNDERSTAND, OR PUPPIES RUNNING ACROSS POLISHED FLOORS AND CRASHING INTO WALLS.

I CAN'T SEE MUCH OF MY ARSE EVEN WITH THE LIGHT ON.

IF YOU DIP IT IN BUTTER FIRST
IT LASTS FOR MORE STROKES.

HEY! IT SAYS HERE I AM DEAD.
I'M NOT DEAD!

CAN WE FIGHT ABOUT IT FIRST?
AND THEN HAVE CONSILIATION SEX?

HAS ONE OF THEM GOT WINGS?

I'M GOING TO DO SOMETHING STRENUOUS AND MASCULINE
LIKE DIGGING AN UNNECESSARILY BIG HOLE.

WHAT IS IT WITH MEN AND DIGGING HOLES?
MY DAD DOES IT AT THE BEACH FOR NO REASON AT ALL.

IF I DIDN'T LIKE HIS WORK SO MUCH
I WOULD KILL HIM AND HAVE HIS WIFE FOR MY VERY OWN.

Do you have any age reducing tips?
Other than smearing semen on my eyelids.

You're marrying your step-dad?
Isn't that a whole therapy session of wrong.

Reformat it and start from scratch.
That's my solution to any awkward software situation. I've probably worn my hard disk flat by now.

He had a sixty year old paunch
squeezed into a twenty year old's leathers

I need age-gaining tips.
Smoking is not 'ageing my skin' like it says on the packet.

Perhaps my anatomy is a little unusual in places.

I love the smell of sexual tension in the morning.

I can't imagine a fly surviving my farts for a three hour journey.

When I think of my dead grandfather
I mostly think about how heavy he was in his coffin. The massive fucker.

I got bored of my cat years ago and had it put to sleep.
No point keeping a cat if you can't be arsed looking after it.

YOU'D HAVE TO CAREFULLY EXPLAIN HOW TO HOLD IT
YOU WOULDN'T WANT IT GOING OFF IN HER FACE.

I'VE JUST HAD A THREE PINT LUNCH
I AM NOW OFFICIALLY **AWESOME**!

I'M GOING TO THE PUB NOW.
TO DRINK BEER WITH OTHER YOUNG MEN AND DISCUSS YOUNG MAN THINGS LIKE TITS AND FOOTBALL AND INVINCIBILITY.

I AM GAMBOLLING THROUGH THE MEADOWS OF MY YOUTH, DEAR. **GAMBOLLING**!

I DON'T WANT TO JOIN IT, I JUST WANT TO ENTER IT.

IT'S WHAT A PENIS DOES
IF ONE IS WEARING OVERALLS WITH NO PANTS AND ISN'T CAREFUL.

TO BE FAIR SHE WAS HYSTERICAL
AND HOLDING A BIG PAIR OF SCISSORS.
I'D HAVE BEEN SLIGHTLY HESITANT ABOUT PHYSICALLY RESTRAINING HER.

CAN YOU TUCK YOUR KNEES INSIDE IT AND HOBBLE ALONG SAYING
"ET PHONE HOME! ET! ET! ET!"

DID IT START OUT WITH HORSEPLAY IN YOUR JIM-JAMS?
PERHAPS A PILLOW FIGHT? OR MAYBE ONE OF YOU WANDERED IN ON THE OTHER IN THE SHOWER AND OFFERED TO HELP WASH THE OTHER ONE'S BACK?

YOU COULDN'T POSSIBLY FIT THAT MANY GOATS IN A CARAVAN.

I CONSIDERED GETTING SOME FOR MY GIRLFRIEND'S VISIT
BUT IT SEEMED VERY DIRTY. NOT SEXY DIRTY, JUST PLAIN UN-HYGIENIC.

DOES ANYONE HAVE ANY TIPS
TO STOP ME WANTING TO KILL MYSELF IN IKEA?

I LIKE MY PRAWNS LIKE MY WOMEN.
FRIED IN GARLIC, AND I HAVE TO PEEL THEM MYSELF.

PARKS ARE BESTEST
EXCEPT IF YOU HAVE TO GO BACK TO THE PUB AND ALL YOUR CLOTHES ARE ALL MUDDY. THEN, IF YOUR MUM STILL WASHES YOUR CLOTHES, YOU HAVE TO DIVIDE THEM UP INTO NON-SUSPICIOUS AMOUNTS AND PUT ONE MUDDY THING IN EACH LOAD FOR A WEEK OR TWO TO BE ON THE SAFE SIDE.

I LIKE TO COMPLETELY FILL MY TROLLEY WITH STUFF
AND THEN DECIDE I DON'T WANT ANY OF IT JUST AS I GET TO THE CHECKOUT.

I HAD TO BUY CONDOMS AND ALSO A PREGNANCY TEST FOR A FRIEND.
THE DISAPPROVING LOOKS FROM THE MIDDLE AGED WOMEN SUGGESTING THAT:
"IT'S A BIT LATE FOR YOU TO START BEING RESPONSIBLE NOW YOUNG MAN"

I AM TOO CHEAP AND OLD TO VISIT NIGHTCLUBS
I JUST GO SHOPPING AT MIDNIGHT WHEN THEY HAVE THE MUSIC ON LOUD AND I CAN DANCE AROUND THE AISLES

I HAVE NEVER FONDLED A BREAST THAT RESEMBLED A BAP IN ANY WAY.
MAYBE I WAS JUST LUCKY AND THEY HAD RUN OUT OF FLOUR.

I AM ALWAYS GETTING INVITED TO PARTIES
MY REALLY CRAP DANCE STEPS MAKE EVERYONE ELSE LOOK GOOD

THE STREETS ARE FULL OF WOMEN WITH ALMOST NO CLOTHES ON,
WANTING TO DO THINGS YOU'VE ONLY DREAMT OF.

MAYBE HE DID GET HIS END AWAY
AND MAYBE SHE WAS RUBBISH AND HE WENT ALL SHRUNKEN AND GOT EMBARRASSED

I SHAVED THEM ONCE, LOOKED LIKE A BLOODFEST AFTER,
NOW I JUST TRIM

SHALL I GO TO THE POST OFFICE FIRST AND THEN THE LIBRARY?
OR LIBRARY FIRST AND THEN POST OFFICE?
IT MAKES NO DIFFERENCE REALLY, I'M JUST WORRIED I'LL GET IT THE WRONG WAY ROUND.

THEY SAY ANTI-DEPRESSANTS MAY CAUSE SUICIDAL THOUGHTS.
I'M LOOKING FORWARD TO SEEING THICKLY-BATTERED ANGINA TABLETS.

I THINK I SHOULD GET GLASSES.
I COULD SHOUT AT PEOPLE AND THEY'D TAKE ME ALL SERIOUS BECAUSE I HAD GLASSES ON.

SOD FATHER CHRISTMAS,
IT'S MY SACK BEING EMPTIED AT THE FOOT OF HER BED.

NO PRIZES FOR GUESSING WHO YOU WOULD LIKE
COMING UP YOUR CHIMNEY THIS CHRISTMAS

DID YOU PULL A CRACKER EARLY?

When I dance at parties people join in
They think I've lost something and help look.

I am leaving stockings at the end of the bed
in the hope they are filled by the time I wake up.

You want to be careful it's not your balls
hanging from the tree Christmas morning.

The old mistletoe hanging from the flies joke
How original.

Champagne and botty sex in bed Christmas morning
One is my treat, the other is his.

Mum, what does "Bloody Wanker" mean?

What's the E.U. ruling about vodka?

You are woman.
This sufferance is the price you have to pay for having tits and being able to get a shag at closing time any night of the week you chose.

I don't know the background to this
so I am going to imagine that you've been cheating on somebody with her own grandmother with hilarious comedy results.

Definitely a man's kitchen,
tin of tuna, out of date mayo jar, beer, empty margarine carton…

REMEMBER, IF EVERYONE ELSE WERE VEGETARIAN
YOU COULD HAVE ALL THE MEAT IN THE WORLD.

JUST GIVE ME A FOOD PROCESSOR
WITH ENOUGH POWER TO CHOP UP STEEL BARS AND AN APRON WITH A PAIR OF KNOCKERS ON THE FRONT OF IT.

I'VE NEVER MET A GOTH I DIDN'T LIKE.
EXCEPT ONE, WHO WAS AN INSIGNIFICANT STATISTICAL ABERRATION.

VICTORIA ALWAYS LOOKED LIKE SHE HAD A COCK UP HER ARSE
AND EMMA WORE SURPRISINGLY SHORT DRESSES FOR ONE SO AMPLE OF THIGH.

THERE WAS NO GORE OR ANYTHING.
JUST FEATHERS AND LEAVES AND GUILT.

I REGULARLY BUY THE WRONG LIGHT BULBS.
THIS MAY CALL FOR A LETTER OF COMPLAINT.

I BUY FRESH GARLIC WHEN I'M COOKING SOMETHING IMPORTANT

I CAN SEE FURTHER IF I STAND ON A BOX.
DOESN'T MEAN EVERYONE IN THE CROWD CAN.

DEALING WITH MONEY IS JUST SOMETHING UTTERLY, UTTERLY DREADFUL
THAT IS **ALWAYS** BETTER DONE TOMORROW.

IF I WERE A BILLIONAIRE
I'D FUND A TIME TRAVELLING JUSTICE SQUAD TO PUT THESE THINGS RIGHT.

EVEN IF YOU *COULD* GO BACK TO 1955,
THERE'D BE NOTHING THERE BECAUSE EVERYTHING IS IN NOW.

MY DEGREE IS IN THEOLOGY.
WHY ON EARTH SHOULD THAT MAKE ME MORE SUITED TO A PROGRAMMING JOB THAN SOMEONE WITH NO DEGREE?

IF YOU TOOK OUT ITEM SEVEN AND THE '**FUCK OFF**' BIT
THAT'D ACTUALLY BE A USEFUL DOCUMENT.

AND WHEN THERE IS NO CHEWABLE FINGERNAIL LEFT,
THE SKIN AROUND IT.

YOU ARE SAYING "ARREST ENOUGH PEOPLE AND YOU'RE BOUND TO GET A TERRORIST"
WHICH IS, SORRY, REALLY STUPID

HOW COME ALL THESE PEOPLE WHO HAVE NEVER SEEN ME NAKED
KNOW EXACTLY HOW I TRIM AND WHAT MY SECRET TATTOO LOOKS LIKE?

IT'S A WORD THAT'S INHERENTLY VERY OFFENSIVE AND RACIST
AND YOU WOULDN'T USE IT UNLESS YOU WANTED TO CAUSE AN EFFECT.

YOU SEEM TO BE REACTING IN A VERY STUPID MANNER
TO A VERY SIMPLE PUT-DOWN OF YOUR RIDICULOUS QUESTION.

I GOT A VOUCHER FOR FREE SPICES FROM ********
FOR WRITING AND COMPLAINING THAT THEIR GARLIC MADE ME STINK LIKE A FRENCHMAN.

I SHALL DESCRIBE IT FOR YOU
USING YMCA-LIKE ARM POSES.

YOU'RE BEING DELIBERATELY THICK.
STOP IT.

IF SHE CARED THAT MUCH
SHE'D HAVE A REAL TOILET INSTALLED.

A PIPE SAVES ME A FORTUNE IN BIROS.

I MADE FRIENDS WITH THIS 75 YEAR OLD MILLIONAIRE CALLED BRUCE
HE CALLED ME HIS 'PRIVATE DANCER'. DON'T ASK.

I FANCY EVERY GIRL UNTIL SHE BECOMES MY GIRLFRIEND.

I DON'T KNOW WHAT HAPPENED,
BUT I WOKE UP WEARING DIFFERENT UNDERWEAR.

WHETHER SOMEONE IS SHIT IS APPARENT EARLIER THAN GIRTH.

I'M FRUSTRATED THAT MY CODE ISN'T WORKING,
BUT AT LEAST I AM

HOW CAN FISH BE BAD PETS?
THEY'RE HARDLY GOING TO CHEW THE CARPETS ARE THEY?

I NEED MORE PUDDING TRAINING MYSELF, REALLY.

THE PITFALL OF ALL PARODY;
YOU BECOME THE THING YOU WERE PARODYING IN THE FIRST PLACE.

HOW DID MY STUPID EYES NOT SEE YOUR INCREDIBLE USELESSNESS.

I'VE WORKED FOR AS MANY YEARS OF MY LIFE
AS THOSE I HAVEN'T. I THINK I MAY NEED TO RETIRE

ARE YOU OFFERING HIM CRACK?
BECAUSE IT'LL NEVER CALM HIM DOWN YOU KNOW

I WOULD HAVE LOVED TO TELL THEM
THAT LESS THAN AN HOUR BEFORE THEY GOT HOME FROM SCHOOL, THEIR MOTHER
WAS WAILING LIKE A JAPANESE PORN STAR AS HER FAT BRUMMY BOYFRIEND
PUMMELED HER RAGGED FOR THE BEST PART OF THE AFTERNOON

WHAT IS RUSTY TROMBONING?

BUT YOUR FACE IS A CANOE
 - OR SOMETHING - JUST BE CAREFUL WITH IT

KICKING A FOREIGN CRACK-ADDICTED SINGLE MUM
OUT OF A COUNCIL FLAT AND GIVING IT TO YOU WOULDN'T SOLVE ANYTHING.

NO NEED TO CHECK UP ON HER HISTORY
IT'S LAID OUT IN DETAIL ON THE BACK OF THE CUBICLE DOORS.

THE DRIVERS DO IT OUT OF BOREDOM I AM SURE,
KEEP SLAMMING ON THE BRAKES COMING INTO A STATION AND SEEING HOW MANY
PEOPLE THEY CAN KNOCK OVER. THEY MUST HAVE A BOOK RUNNING

YOU KNOW WHEN THE THOUGHT GOES THROUGH YOUR HEAD
THAT YOU PROBABLY SHOULDN'T BE DOING IT? I IGNORED THAT THOUGHT.

I'M GREAT AT TUBE RIDING
I'M BLESSED WITH BOINGY KNEES

WHAT PART OF THE CHICKEN DOES THAT COME FROM EXACTLY?

HAD IT ONCE IN LONDON
CANT GET IT UP IN BRUM.

KICK ONE OF THEM OUT - PREFERABLY YOUR SECRETARY,
'COS I RECKON THE GRAD STUDENT PROBABLY SHAGS INFINITELY BETTER.

I HAVE DECIDED THE ONLY PARTICIPATION I AM MAKING IN THE MOVE
IS TO CLIMB INTO THE BIGGEST BOX AND WAIT FOR IT ALL TO HAPPEN AROUND ME.

MY HEAD FEELS LIKE A STEAMROLLER WENT OVER IT
AND I'M NOT GOING FAR FROM THE BATHROOM TODAY.

SHE MAY BE HOT, BUT FUCK ME, SHE DRONES ON.

SEEING AS I'VE ALREADY PURCHASED THE POT NOODLES
YOGURT IS HARDLY GOING TO BE CHEAPER NOW IS IT?

POT FUCKING NOODLES?
WHY NOT JUST EMPTY THE CONTENTS OF YOUR HOOVER BAG INTO A CUP AND ADD
BOILING WATER? SAME THING BUT CHEAPER.

HER HEAD'S SO BIG,
WHEN SHE'S HOSTING SOMETHING ON ITV YOU CAN SEE HER EARS ON BBC2 AND C4.

I'M IN THE MOOD TO BE TAKEN ADVANTAGE OF.

ALL IT NEEDS
IS A CLAP OF THUNDER AND A WOMAN'S SCREAM TO MAKE IT COMPLETE

I AM WAITING FOR THE KIDS TO PISS OFF TO A PARTY
SO I CAN GO AND ENJOY MYSELF WITHOUT HAVING TO PAY FOR THEM AS WELL.

THE ONLY STRIP CLUBS ONE SHOULD GO TO ARE
THE ONES WHERE YOU CAN HAVE A DRINK, AND THEN IF YOU WANT TO SEE SOME
BREASTS, YOU JUST TURN YOUR HEAD TOWARD THE STAGE, THEN BACK TO YOUR DRINK
AGAIN AFTER NODDING APPROVINGLY.

SHE SAYS SHE TRIPPED AND FELL DOWN THE STAIRS -
THOSE FIST SIZED BRUISES ARE PURE COINCIDENCE

KEEP THAT STRAP-ON AWAY FROM ME.
I DON'T LIKE THE GLINT IN YOUR EYE.

TOO MANY TOPICS
COGNITIVE OVERLOAD

MY HOUSEMATE HAS A NEW GIRLFRIEND
SO WE WILL HAVE TO LISTEN TO HIM BANGING AWAY UNTIL THE EARLY HOURS AGAIN.
PERHAPS I SHOULD BURST INTO HIS ROOM AND ASK WHY HE IS CHEATING ON ME.
DOUBLE WHAMMY, SHE THINKS HE IS CHEATING AND GAY IN ONE MOVE.

NOTHING COULD BE WORSE THAN HAVING ON YOUR BIRTH CERTIFICATE:
"PLACE OF BIRTH: BIRMINGHAM"

FEMALES ARE FOR GAYS
CARS ARE WHERE ITS AT.

IF YOU LET THAT WOMAN RUN YOUR LIFE NOW,
YOU'RE FUCKED FOR ETERNITY...

IF THEY'RE THIS BAD NOW JUST THINK OF WHEN THEY'RE GROWN UP.

ISN'T IT FOUR TIMES THE LENGTH OF THE BODY?

I DIDN'T COP A FEEL
BUT I DID FEEL HER MASSIVE TITS AGAINST MY CHEST WHEN WE DID THE FOXTROT

I'M GOING TO STOP ASKING QUESTIONS I DON'T WANT TO KNOW THE ANSWERS TO

CHRIST, THREE HOURS JUST HAPPENED,
ONLY I'M NOT SURE WHAT HAPPENED... AND THIS PROBABLY ISN'T THE FIRST TIME THIS WEEK THIS HAS HAPPENED.

FREEDOM OF CHOICE?
THIS GOVERNMENT HAS PUT PAID TO THAT.

IT'S ALWAYS 'LARGER' PEOPLE WHO BRING IT UP I FIND
I HAVE NEVER SEEN A SLIM GIRL COMPLAIN THAT MEN HATE SKINNY GIRLS.

WOMEN ALWAYS THINK THEY ARE LARGER THAN THEY ARE,
AND MEN THINK THEY'RE ONLY TEN PRESS-UPS AWAY FROM PERFECTION.

MY CURRENT CHOICES IN LIFE STRONGLY INDICATE I WILL NEVER
BECOME ONE.

WE HONESTLY DIDN'T NOTICE SHE WAS SO PISSED
UNTIL SHE FELL OFF HER CHAIR

I REMEMBER THROWING UP PINK SICK

THE BIBLE IS NOT FULL OF CONSPIRACY THEORIES ABOUT JESUS.

SHE FIRST TOLD ME SHE WAS 23, WHICH BECAME 21 AFTER SLAMMERS.
LATER, IN BED SHE CONFESSED SHE WAS REALLY ONLY 19. I SNUCK OUT THIS
MORNING BEFORE SHE COULD OPEN HER MOUTH AND PUT ME AWAY FOR 5 YEARS.

LUCKILY,
I FOUND OUT SHE WAS A LESBIAN BEFORE I BOUGHT HER A DRINK.

THAT IS LIKE SAYING
A CREAM CAKE IS BETTER THAN DROWNING IN DOG TURD.

THE BAD GRAMMAR IN THIS SONG HAS ALWAYS BOTHERED ME
ALTHOUGH I'M NOT SURE IT'S HEALTHY TO WORRY ABOUT GRAMMAR IN MUSIC.

REMEMBER THE OLD ADAGE:
WINE THEN BEER MAKES YOU FEEL QUEER

I WAS A SIZE 18-20 A WHILE AGO.
NOW I'M SIZE 10-12 THE LEVEL OF INTEREST HASN'T REALLY CHANGED. JUST
DIFFERENT PEOPLE ASKING FOR DIFFERENT THINGS.

I'M NOT DRUNK
I'M JUST ANNOYING

I'M GOING TO THE FARMERS' MARKET FOR ALL MY SPIRITUAL NEEDS.
I'M IN A PORK AND CHEESE MOOD TODAY

I DON'T KNOW WHAT ANY OF THAT MEANS
SO I'LL JUST SIT HERE QUIETLY

YOU'D THINK WHAT WITH IT BEING CALLED "THE JOLLY SAILOR"
I MIGHT'VE HAD AN INKLING OF WHAT I WAS LETTING MYSELF IN FOR BEFOREHAND.

I BLAME NIGEL AND HIS HOMEMADE SLOE VODKA.
MORE FOOL HIM THOUGH, HE'S GOT WORK TODAY

I WAS HOPING WE'D GET SOME NICHE PORN
WITH A DISTINCTLY BRITISH BENT.

JUST BECAUSE THEY MAKE IT IN A CERTAIN SIZE,
DOESN'T MEAN YOU SHOULD WEAR IT.

LYCRA AND BREASTS ARE VERY RARELY A BAD COMBINATION.
LYCRA AND BUTTOCKS IS A WHOLE DIFFERENT STORY.

IT'S PROBABLY BECAUSE MY UNDERPANTS ARE A LITTLE SNUG

I PARTICULARLY LIKE SEEING THE BACK OF A WOMAN'S HEAD
IF YOU KNOW WHAT I MEAN.

ONE DAY WE WILL FIND OUT THE TRUTH
WHEN THOSE RESPONSIBLE ARE DEAD, OR TOO OLD TO BE HELD ACCOUNTABLE.

YOU WANT WHAT WE ALL WANT - TO BE LOVED -
-TO BE LOVED AND HUMPED AT THE SAME TIME. I'M HERE IF EVER YOU NEED ME.

SHE SAID "I LIKE BEING WOKEN IN THE MIDDLE OF THE NIGHT FOR SEX"
I STUPIDLY BELIEVED HER.

FORGET THE MEAL
LET'S JUST SKIP STRAIGHT TO THE SPANKING AND THE ORAL SEX

WHAT WOMAN DOESN'T LOOK GOOD IN HEAD-TO-TOE BLACK?

I'M NOT PREGNANT I'VE JUST GOT BIG TITS!

TOO MUCH DUNKING MAKES IT GO SOGGY AND DROP OFF, YOU KNOW.

DOES SOCIOPHOBE MEAN YOU DON'T DO GROUP SEX?

I HAD TO RAPE HIM UNTIL HE WAS NEARLY DEAD..
AND JUDGING FROM THE TEXTS SINCE HE HAD TO GO HOME, HE WANTS MORE RAPAGE

SPEAKING FOR **ONE** MILLISECOND ON THE ORAL SEX..
HE WAS ERR.. OK I'LL SHUT UP BUT I CAN COME AGAIN.. NO I MEAN HE CAN..
AHAHAHA

SHE TOLD ME SHE HAD DONE THE **BEST** AND THE **WORST** THING EVER.
I GUESSED IT WAS 'DOUBLE PENETRATION'. SHE DID NOT SEE THE FUNNY SIDE.

MEN ARE LIKE TOILETS,
FULL OF SHIT

I'M WONDERING IF IT HAS ANYTHING TO DO WITH A CLEVELAND STEAMER

YOUR BREASTS ARE INCREDIBLY SMOOTH,
DO YOU SHAVE?

DID YOU JUST LUNGE AT MY CLUNGE?

I'VE NOT SEEN HIM RECENTLY,
HAS HE GONE ALL POSTAL AND SHOT HIMSELF?

WELL, I HAVEN'T DRESSED UP TONIGHT,
YOU'D PROBABLY THINK I WAS GOOD LOOKING IF I HAD DRESSED UP.

I'VE HEARD THE RUMOURS,
AND I'M NOW CALLING THE ST. JOHNS, SAMARITANS AND THE RSPCA.

I CRIED WHEN SPIKE DIED, LIKE A BIG GIRL.
OF COURSE, I WAS IN THE DEPTHS OF DEPRESSION AT THE TIME.

WHEN I WAS A CHILD
WE CALLED FANNIES "HENNY PENNYS"

HAVE YOU NEVER CONSIDERED A PERSONAL TRIM?

A BOIL ON YOUR WILLY?
HAVE YOU BEEN DOWN NAUGHTY NELLY'S KNOCKING SHOP AGAIN?

LIGHTLY SAUTEED WITH GARLIC UNTIL TRANSPARENT AND SOFTENED,
SEASONED WELL WITH SEA SALT AND BLACK PEPPER, DOUSED IN BRANDY, THEN
FLAMBEED TO A CRISP AND THROWN IN THE BIN.

I USED TO GIVE MY ADDRESS TO MEN ONLINE
THEN I WOULD UNLOCK MY DOOR AND GO TO BED.

I COULD ONLY BE MORE MANLY IF I STIRRED BARBECUE COALS WITH MY
PENIS.

I AM NEVER DEPRESSED WHEN DRINKING
WHEN REALITY KICKS IN IS A WHOLE DIFFERENT STORY

IF I KNEW I WAS TO DIE TOMORROW
I WOULD SHAG THE NEAREST FIT GUY, RUN DRUNK AND NAKED DOWN THE STREET,
CUM RUNNING DOWN MY THIGHS, AND GET ARRESTED. ISN'T IT SAD HOW WE CAN'T DO
THE THINGS WE REALLY WANT TO DO UNTIL IT'S TOO LATE?

I MAKE LOVE TO MY WIFE FROM BEHIND
SHE CAN IMAGINE I AM ANY MAN SHE HAS FANCIED THAT DAY AND I DON'T HAVE TO
LOOK AT HER FACE.

YOU DON'T KNOW SOMEONE TILL YOU'VE LIVED WITH THEM

LIFE IS SIMPLE,
UNLESS YOU CHOOSE TO MAKE IT COMPLICATED BY GETTING TOO ATTACHED TO
THINGS.

I CORRUPTED THE INNOCENCE OF A SMALL CHILD
DUE TO A HIGH WIND AND A POORLY-TIED DRESSING GOWN.

DINNER WAS LIKE MY EX
COLD, UNSATISFYING AND EXPENSIVE.

WE PREFER THE TERM 'SURPRISE SEX'

YOU POOR SOD.
I COULD ALMOST HEAR YOUR HEART BOTH STOP AND START FROM HERE

I THINK YOU'RE DOING IT THE WRONG WAY

YOUR HEAD IS TOO BIG TO FIT DOWN THERE.

ROCKING HORSE POO IS RARER THAN CHICKEN'S TEETH

THEY WERE CHILD ACTRESSES, AND NOW THEY SUCK?
IT SOUNDS LIKE A NATURAL CAREER PROGRESSION THESE DAYS.

I SNEEZED SPUNK ONCE.
NOT AN ENTIRELY PLEASANT EXPERIENCE, THOUGH IT MADE ME LAUGH LIKE A DRAIN.

WAKE HER UP BY SUDDENLY SHOUTING
'QUICK MS FRANK, THE GESTAPO IS COMING!'

I DON'T HAVE AN INFERIORITY COMPLEX ABOUT MY GRAPHICS CARD
BUT I DO LIVE WITH MY PARENTS.

My daughter did in fact once say 'Daddy tastes good'.

My beer is empty right now,
an unacceptable lapse on my part.

I do remember what you look like...
fat, ugly, so yes, perfectly...
No, I am not looking in a fucking mirror!

It started off with wifey's 'extreme hoovering' in the wee hours,
and has gone progressively downhill since.

'Fastening a woggle' sounds much dirtier than 'touching a penis'

England can't do any sport
except perhaps world championship beer drinking

I am over-the-limit, over-the-hill, over-weight and over here.

Trimming the bikini line with shears
was always going to be fraught with danger

I'm not gay,
but I've shagged a bloke who is

I'm a chick magnet
Hang out with me and you can have 50% of all chicks I pull.

A FEW MORE CANDLES ON YOUR CAKE
AND YOU'LL BE LEGAL.

I'M GOOD AT BEING THE UGLY FRIEND
WHO MAKES EVERYONE ELSE FEEL ATTRACTIVE.

DOES THIS EXERCISING INCLUDE FOOD PER CHANCE?

IF THE WORLD WERE TO END TOMORROW, YOU CAN'T GO WRONG WITH A BIT OF COCK.
BUT I'D PROBABLY INTERSPERSE IT WITH SOME CHOCOLATE AND SINGING AT THE TOP OF MY VOICE AND RUNNING NAKED THROUGH THE STREETS

YES, BARNSLEY.
WHERE MEN ARE MEN, AND SO ARE THE WOMEN.

FOR SOMEONE SO CUTE AND DIMPLY
YOU CAN BE AMUSINGLY CRUDE SOMETIMES

THANK HEAVENS FOR THE GAG REFLEX

MY FRIEND'S DAD IS A CROSS-DRESSING WEIRDO,
I CAN DEFINITELY SAY YOU CAN'T TELL IF SOMEONE IS GAY BY THE WAY THEY LOOK.

I HAVE MISSED YOUR IMPECCABLE DRESS SENSE,
YOUR FRIENDLY FACE AND YOUR FILTHY MOUTH.

MOST WOMEN ARE A LITTLE BI-SEXUAL, BUT I'M TRI-SEXUAL.
I'LL TRY ANYTHING ONCE

WOMEN LIKE TO BULLY ME
BY NOT ENGAGING IN SEXUAL INTERCOURSE.

I CAN TELL JUST BY LOOKING. I'M ALWAYS RIGHT.
I'VE PROBABLY GOT A CORRECT AVERAGE OF ABOUT 80%

SHE'LL NEVER GET YOU PREGNANT
NOT MATTER HOW BUTCH SHE IS

I'M A BIT BAD WHEN I'M DRUNK, I'LL FLIRT WITH ANYONE.
WHICH ONE OF YOU GENTLEMEN WILL BUY ME A DRINK?

AS I WAS TRIMMING MY FINGERNAILS
IT OCCURRED TO ME THAT I COULD NOT DO MY JOB WITH LONG FINGERNAILS AND
THUS, IN MY OWN SMALL WAY, I WAS MODIFYING MY BODY FOR MY EMPLOYER.

POO, POO, BARNEY'S A JEW, CUSTARD, DRIBBLE AND SNOT

WHEN THE HOT RUSSIAN IS IN,
SITTING AT MY DESK AND DROOLING IS ALL I CAN MANAGE.

A SMALL HARD DRIVE INSERTED INTO MY HEAD MIGHT BE GOOD,
I HAVE A FUCKING AWFUL MEMORY

I'M HAVING SOME PROBLEMS I NEED YOU TO LOOK AT.

AND BEST SPOKEN
WHILE CLAPPING THE WRONG SIDE OF YOUR HANDS TOGETHER

I DOUBT HE IS UP TO HIS NUTS IN A BETTER LOOKING GIRL THAN YOU RIGHT NOW.
THAT PROBABLY DIDN'T HELP REALLY, DID IT.

IF YOU WEREN'T SO FUNNY YOU'D BE A WASTE OF SKIN.

MY ANUS ALREADY SPORTS BEADS OF SWEAT
EACH TIME I THINK OF YOU

A BRAIN WOULD BE NICE
BUT YOU CAN DO MY JOB WITHOUT ONE.

BUT YOU'RE NOT FRISKY, OR YOUNG, OR SAUCY.

YOU MAY BE RIGHT, THEY MAY NOT ACTUALLY BE LOVE BALLS,
BUT ALL THE SAME I THINK YOU'LL FIND IT WAS YOU WHO DROPPED THEM.

I GOT MARRIED TOO SOON,
AND TO THE WRONG PERSON. AND FOR THE WRONG REASON. AND FOR TOO MUCH MONEY

I THINK THE TRICK IS TO WAIT TILL YOU'RE WELL INTO YOUR THIRTIES.
THEN YOU'RE NOT ONLY SANE ENOUGH TO DECIDE, BUT YOU'VE ALSO SPENT THE PAST FIFTEEN YEARS ENJOYING DEBAUCHERY AND YOU'RE READY FOR A BIT OF MONOGAMY.

AN EYE IN THE BACK OF MY HEAD
SO I CAN SEE WHERE I'M WENTING FROM AS WELL AS WHERE I'M COMING AGAINST.

A BASEBALL CAP WITH REAR VIEW MIRRORS
USEFUL AND TRENDY.

A BEARD WITH NO MOUSTACHE IS JUST WRONG

I WENT OUT WITH A COUPLE OF ART COLLEGE TYPE GIRLS.
THEY TALKED ABOUT WANKING WITH DOORKNOBS AT PUBLIC SCHOOL AND STILL
MANAGED TO MAKE IT SOUND TEDIOUS.

A KNOB OF BUTTER OR KNOB BUTTER.
BIG DIFFERENCE I THINK YOU'LL FIND.

WHAT A COINCIDENCE
I LOVE ME TOO

IF YOU COULD BREED HIM WITH A DOG
YOU'D HAVE A PERFECT OBEDIENT SEX PET.

YOU'RE THINKING ABOUT HER RIGHT NOW, AREN'T YOU?
NAKED. I CAN TELL.

MY BEARD IS GINGER
BUT IT'S A SECRET

I GET MISTAKEN FOR SOMEONE WORKING AT VIRGIN RECORDS.
DO I REALLY LOOK LIKE I KNOW MY WAY ROUND THE JAZZ SECTION?

STRAIGHT, THIN, HARDWORKING, SEXUALLY NORMAL AND ADJUSTED.
OR SHOULD I JUST PUT DOWN THE TRUTH?

IT REMINDS ME OF THE HAPPY TIME I WAS MISTAKEN FOR A CELEBRITY
AND HAD MY PHOTO TAKEN WITH LOTS OF PORN ACTRESSES

INSTEAD OF MALE GEEKY INTERNET NERDS, THEY WERE SEXY GIRLS...
WELL, NOT REALLY SEXY, BUT NAKED.

I LIKE A GIRL WITH SPUNK INSIDE HER.

GET THEE TO THE SUPERMARKET
BUY YOURSELF A BOTTLE OF GIN, A TUB OF LUBE AND A CUCUMBER.
MEN ARE SHIT.

IS THAT LIKE A 69
BUT LEANING AGAINST A WALL?

WHAT?! THE BANG BUS ISN'T REAL?

SCAT IS SOME SERIOUSLY FUCKED UP SHIT

PUT THAT BACK.
IT SHOULDN'T BE OUT THIS TIME OF DAY.

MY WIFE WENT AND TOLD HER MOTHER THAT I COULDN'T GET IT UP.
TROUBLE IS, HER MOTHER KNOWS I CAN AND ARGUED MY CASE WITHOUT THINKING.
I AM IN DEEP SHIT NOW.

I WRITE STORIES ON THE WALL JUST BEFORE I WALLPAPER.
IN 100 YEARS TIME SOME POOR BASTARD IS GOING TO REALISE THAT A MADMAN
LIVED IN THE HOUSE BEFORE HIM AND WORRY THAT BODIES ARE BURIED UNDER THE
100 YEAR OLD PATIO.

I WAS NOT PREPARED FOR THAT STATEMENT MENTALLY OR OTHERWISE.

IF I DON'T GET THE JOB
I'LL JUST FIND SOME RICH GUY AND MAKE SURE I GET PREGNANT THIS TIME.

THE FILLING IN YOUR PANTS
IS NOT FILLING ME WITH ANYTHING I CAN ASSURE YOU

I HAVE MANY OPINIONS ON SCHOOL UNIFORMS ON GROWN WOMEN
ALL OF THEM GOOD

24 IS THE OPTIMUM AGE TO START HAVING CHILDREN
WOULD YOU LIKE TO START NOW?

THE SWEATINESS
ACTUALLY MAKES IT EASIER TO GET THE FLACID MEMBER IN.

THEY JUST LIE THERE MOANING
AND NOT IN A NICE WAY

THAT MAGIC AGE
WHERE YOU SUDDENLY FIND YOURSELF TOO OLD FOR YOUNG GUYS, AND TOO OLD FOR OLD GUYS.

IT'S NOT COMING OFF, IT'S TOO STICKY
YOU'LL HAVE TO SUCK IT OFF I'M AFRAID

I'VE SEEN THAT HAPPEN BEFORE,
I LAUGH AND FEEL SORRY AT THE SAME TIME.

MY DAD GOT ORAL THRUSH WHEN HE WAS ABOUT 65
I DIDN'T ASK HOW

I HATE PEOPLE WHO PUT THEIR STUFF ON SEATS ON BUSY TRAINS
THEN LOOK LIKE I'VE ASKED TO FUCK THEIR CHILDREN WHEN I WANT TO SIT DOWN

WHEN A MAN IS TIRED OF BEER
HE IS TIRED OF LIFE

MY EX RUSHED IN TO DO A NUMBER 2 ONCE WHILE I WAS IN THE BATH.
I WAS NOT BEST PLEASED

HE SAID HE HADN'T HAD A DRINK IN ELEVEN YEARS.
HE MUST BE BLOODY THIRSTY

I KNOW YOU ASKED ME NEVER TO TELL ANYONE.

I FIND POSH GIRLS ARE MORE LIKELY TO SAY YES TO ANYTHING,

POSH GIRLS DON'T COME, THEY ARRIVE

PIPPA FROM THE PONY CLUB,
LOOKS LIKE A HORSE, SMELLS LIKE A HORSE, GOES LIKE A THOROUGHBRED!

DOGGY STYLE,
THE MAN BEGS FOR IT WHILE THE WOMAN ROLLS OVER AND PLAYS DEAD.

I NEVER TRUST ANYONE THAT DOESN'T DRINK
THEY REMEMBER EVERYTHING I SAID AND DID THE NEXT DAY

I BE TRYING TO LOSE A LITTLE WEIGHT AT THE MOMENT,
SO I'M EATING VERY QUICKLY.

I WAS CONVINCED I COULD SEE THE FACE OF GOD IN THE MICROWAVE.
TOOK ME HALF AN HOUR TO WORK UP THE COURAGE TO GO AND INVESTIGATE.
IT WAS A BUCKET OF KFC.

BURN IT,
THEN BURY THE ASHES AND HEAVILY SALT THE EARTH AFTERWARDS

PERHAPS YOU HAVE HEAVY FEET.

OUR MARRIAGE VOWS WERE; 'TO LOVE, HONOUR AND TOLERATE'
TO LOVE, HONOUR AND IGNORE WOULD HAVE BEEN MORE ACCURATE

THE ONLY REASON YOU ARE VEGETARIAN
IS SO YOU HAVE ANOTHER THING YOU CAN WHINE ABOUT.

I GOT DRUNK AT MY BOSSES HOUSE CHRISTMAS PARTY,
I HAD BEEN SITTING ON THE LOO. HE CAME IN AND SAW MY BUM AS I WAS LEANT OVER THE BATH TO VOMIT. AS IF HIM SEEING ME VOMIT WAS NOT BAD ENOUGH ON IT'S OWN.

I LIKE TO CATCH A WOMAN'S EYE AS SHE IS SELECTING A CUCUMBER.
THE LOOK IN HER EYES SAYS IT ALL. SHE IS USING A SYSTEM OF SELECTION THAT IS NOT ALTOGETHER THE ONE SHE WOULD CARE TO ADMIT TO.

HE WAS NAKED IN FRONT OF THE WINDOW JUMPING UP AND DOWN
MAKING THE 'WOOO WOOO' SOUND WHILE IT SLAPPED OFF HIS BELLY.

THOSE WOMEN ARE UP FOR ANYTHING
ONCE THE STRIPPER GETS HIS DICK OUT

I WENT TO THE DOCTORS AND SHOWED HIM SOMETHING THIS MORNING
WHEN HE FINALLY STOPPED LAUGHING HE GAVE ME SOME PILLS.

I WENT TO A POSH SCHOOL
WHERE THE GIRLS WOULDN'T PUT OUT FOR LESS THAN A PORSCHE. SO WE USED TO SNEAK TO THE LOCAL COUNCIL ESTATE WHERE THE GIRLS WOULD FUCK YOU FOR A BOTTLE OF CIDER.

YOU WERE SUPPOSED TO TEXT REQUESTS TO THE DJ
BY TEXTING THE WORD "REQUEST" AND THEN YOUR SONG TITLE.
PREDICTIVE TEXT MADE ME SEND THE WORD "PERVERT" INSTEAD.

HE'S VERY POSH
WHEN HE HAS AN ORGASM HE GOES 'OH...OHH...OHHH, RATHER!'

I TOLD MY WIFE HER ARSE LOOKED BIG IN THIS PAIR OF JEANS ONCE, AND HOW LOVELY SHE LOOKED 100 OTHER TIMES. GUESS WHICH SHE REMEMBERS?

PLEASE COME AND AGGRESSIVELY TAKE THEM OUT ON MY HOUSEMATE
I'LL DENY EVER MEETING YOU

DRUNK MYSELF STUPID AND ACCEPTED A FUCK-OFF TWO HANDED JOINT
THEN I WAS PASSING OUT AND BEING VIOLENTLY SICK ALL AT THE SAME TIME.
I ALMOST DIED FROM VOMIT INHALATION.
THEN I FELL ON A FIRE WHICH DIDN'T IMPROVE MATTERS ANYWHAT.

I'VE BEEN THROUGH THE DESERT ON A HORSE WITH NO LEGS
- TOOK FUCKING AGES.

A GOOD SET OF BRASS KNUCKLES AND STEEL TOECAPS NEVER DID ANYONE ANY HARM.

YOU'RE STILL A MASSIVE SLACK-FANNIED BUSHPIG THOUGH

I WAS SO STONED
I RANG THE POLICE AND REPORTED MY FLATMATE FOR STEALING MY STASH OF WEED

I DON'T EAT MEAT
I HAVE BEEN KNOWN TO SUCK ON A KEBAB AND SPIT IT OUT THOUGH

DOES THIS SMELL OF CHLOROFORM TO YOU?

LETS HAVE WILD TORRID SEX ON THE BONNET OF YOUR SPORTS CAR
TO THE TUNE OF POUR SOME SUGAR ON ME.

PREGNANT WIVES ON TOP ARE GREAT.
IT'S WORTH HAVING CHILDREN FOR.

FIRST CYCLING OF THE YEAR,
ARSE FEELS LIKE IT HAS GONE TEN ROUNDS AT A PRISON PARTY.

I JUST ORDERED A TEACAKE.
BUT IT WASN'T A CAKE AND IT CONTAINED NO TEA.

BRILLIANT THUNDER LAST NIGHT,
I HAD A BED FULL OF QUAKING FEMALES. IT WAS LIKE SOUND OF MUSIC ON STEROIDS.

I MADE A LADY ON THE 8.34 TO WATERLOO HAPPY TODAY
WHEN THE TRAIN UNEXPECTEDLY LURCHED AND I GRABBED HER BREAST TO STEADY MYSELF.

SO WHO HAS THE MISSING TRILLIONS WE ARE ALL HAVING TO PAY?
I SURE WOULD LIKE TO MEET THEM.

WHAT I REALLY NEED NOW IS SOME SLEEP
AND TO FIND MY UNDERWEAR.

MUMMY, I SAW A CALF STUCK UP A COW'S BOTTOM

THEY SAY YOUR WHOLE LIFE FLASHES BEFORE YOUR EYES
BUT I SWEAR IT WAS A BIG RED BUS

HOW COME YOU WAKE UP NEXT TO A BEAUTIFUL BRAZILLIAN MODEL
AND I WAKE UP TO FIND A COLD KEBAB WITH EXTRA CHILLI SAUCE?

A TUBE OF KY AND A BOTTLE OF THE FIZZY PANTY REMOVER PLEASE

WE WEREN'T TOGETHER FOR LONG, THANK GOD,
SHE CAME AT ME WITH SCISSORS A FEW TIMES, WENT ON ABOUT THROWING HERSELF DOWN THE STAIRS, HITTING ME, ALL THE USUAL STUFF. THEN SHE BROKE UP WITH ME BECAUSE SHE SAID I WAS NUTS.

LAID OUT ARTWORK FOR NEW BOOK READY TO GO FOR PROOFING.
IT'S AN AMUSING TRAVELLING COMPANION OF A BOOK ABOUT SOHO. NOW FOR THE PUB TO PONDER WHERE THE NEXT BOOK SHOULD BE BASED.

THE END

www.ingramcontent.com/pod-product-compliance
Lightning Source LLC
Chambersburg PA
CBHW020802160426
43192CB00006B/408